OPEN ROAD'S BEST OF

Paris

by Andy Herbach

Open Road Travel Guides – designed for the amount of time you *really* have for your trip!

Open Road Publishing

Open Road's new travel guides.
Designed to cut to the chase.
You don't need a huge travel encyclopedia – you need a *selective guide*
to steer you right. If you're going on vacation for a few weeks or less,
get a guide that brings you the *best* of any destination for the amount
of time you *really* have for your trip!

Open Road – the guide you need for the trip you want.

The New Open Road *Best Of* Travel Guides.
Right to the point.
Uncluttered.
Easy.

Open Road Publishing
P.O. Box 284, Cold Spring Harbor, NY 11724
www.openroadguides.com

Text Copyright © 2007 by Andy Herbach
- All Rights Reserved -
ISBN 1-59360-095-X
Library of Congress Control No. 2007923358

About the Author

Andy Herbach is also the author of *Open Road's Best of Provence*,
Open Road's Best of Spain, *Eating & Drinking in Paris* (co-author),
Europe Made Easy, *Paris Made Easy*, *Berlin Made Easy*, and
Amsterdam Made Easy. All of Andy's books and other great
travel info can be found on his website: www.eatndrink.com.

CONTENTS

Your Passport to the **Perfect Trip!**

6. GREAT WALKS IN PARIS 129

Highlights: do-it-yourself walking tours with street by street directions

7. BEST SLEEPS & EATS 165

Highlights: the best hotels and restaurants in different price ranges

8. BEST ACTIVITIES   194

Highlights: great shopping, terrific nightlife, and a fun variety of sports and recreation

Maps

PHOTO CREDITS

The following photos are from Shutterstock.com: front cover photo, and pp. 13top, 18, 26, 53, 58, 61top, 96 bottom, 101, 104, 137, 148, 160, 201. *The following photos are by Karl Raaum*: back cover, 77, 162, 189, 190, 197. *The following images are from flickr.com*: p. 3 (cafe): daviddesign; pp. 19: gordieryan; pp. 20, 108, 216: Jef Poskanzer; pp. 22: Fenners1984; pp. 23, 100, 214: Joe Shlabotnik; pp. 24, 121, 214: Tomoyoshi; pp. 25, 144: gigi4791; pp. 30, 59, 105, 149: ivalladt; p. 31: psd; p. 32: metropol2; p. 36: Erman Miami; p. 37: vantan; p. 38: alterednate; p. 39: Ronny H; p. 42: innusa; p. 44: Rebekah Travis; p. 45: EJFinneranJr; p. 46: Ashley Duffus; p. 47: Dirk Auerbach; p. 3 top, 49: createsimona; p. 50 left: karneyli; p. 50 right: michone; p. 52: andresso; p. 55: Reggie Goh; pp. 56: Golden Wolf 444; p. 57: Rita Crane (www.ritacranestudio.com); p. 61 bottom: billandkent; pp. 6, 1595: petursey; p. 67: maarten18; pp. 71, 95: sheilaellen; pp. 72, 102, 113, 158: Daquella manera; p. 73: stofoto; p. 75: edwin11_79; pp. 83, 153, 218: robertpaulyoung; p. 84: billandkent; p. 85: talkrhubarb; p. 87: Lieve Kat; p. 89: Juliette Lelchuk; p. 92: Sujith Chandran; p. 93: David Sifry; p. 96 top: JimmyOK; p. 97 left: sergeymk; p. 97 right: artandscience; p. 107: saragoldsmith; p. 111: beggs; p. 114 top: martius; p. 114 bottom: King Coyote; p. 118: extranoise; p. 123: David Perez Facorro; p. 124: Grébert; p. 125: luisvilla; p. 128 top: Neil Rickards; p. 128 bottom: Boss Tweed; p. 129: Kelvin Wright; p. 132: james.; p. 136: Wolfiewolf; p. 138: Jez; p. 139: La case photo de Got; p. 150: Garrulus; pp. 155, 177: gadjoboy; p. 156: firepile; p. 161: XenMantra; p. 163: Rui Ornelas; p. 164: pedrosimoes7; p. 165: jurveston; p. 170: Foraggio; p. 172: gromgull; p. 180: MorganeC/Hotels Paris Rive Gauche; p. 182: misa_; p. 187: dobsohn; p. 191 top: malias; p. 191 bottom: Sara Good Lucks; p. 192: Li Jen Kuo; p. 194: Tony Allen-Mills; p. 197: mteson; p. 203: saudi; p. 204: John Cohen; p. 205: denisparis; p. 207: El Mostrito; p. 208: mshamma; p. 211: ehengel; p. 213: bubble_gum; p. 217: thombo2; p. 222: Kit Hartford; p. 223: MikeandKim; p. 227: SkyCandy. Note: the use of these photos does not represent an endorsement of this book or any services listed within by any of the photographers listed above.

ACKNOWLEDGMENTS

French editor: Marie Fossier. English editors: Jonathan Stein and Marian Olson. Contributor: Karl Raaum. Additional research: Mark Berry, Dan Schmidt, Jeff Kurz, Jim Mortell, Trish Medalen, and Terry Medalen

1. INTRODUCTION

Paris is the most fabulous city in the world, not because of the Eiffel Tower or the Champs-Élysées, but because there's simply no other place in the world like it.

It's called the City of Light, but perhaps it should be called the City of Promise. Around every corner is the promise of another beautiful street, another bistro filled with people eating delicious food (Paris is a city where you have to work at having a bad meal), another building that in any other city would be remarkable, but in Paris is just another building. Walk down practically any block in Paris, and the sights, smells and sounds will excite you.

With this book you'll have the **best of Paris** at your fingertips, from the familiar Arc de Triomphe to the unusual Anatomy Museum, with tips on the best places to eat, sleep and shop.

This guide covers all the information you need to plan a day, a weekend, or even more in Paris without burdening you with a long list of options that simply aren't worth your precious vacation time. Just take off and enjoy–you've got a great adventure ahead!

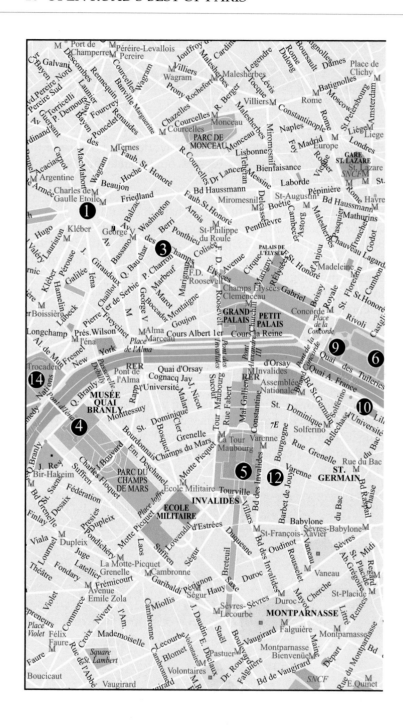

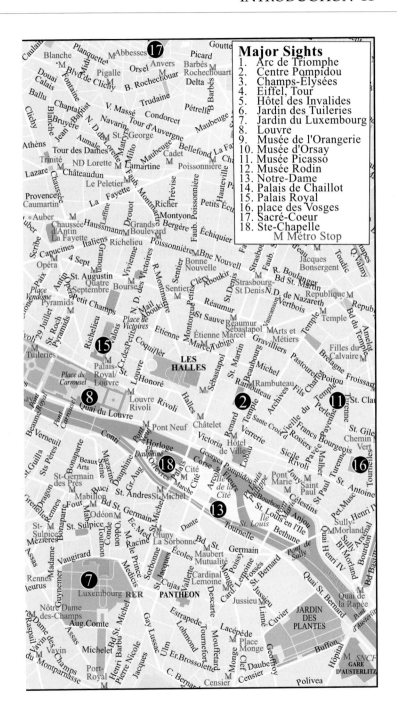

Major Sights
1. Arc de Triomphe
2. Centre Pompidou
3. Champs-Elysées
4. Eiffel, Tour
5. Hôtel des Invalides
6. Jardin des Tuileries
7. Jardin du Luxembourg
8. Louvre
9. Musée de l'Orangerie
10. Musée d'Orsay
11. Musée Picasso
12. Musée Rodin
13. Notre-Dame
14. Palais de Chaillot
15. Palais Royal
16. place des Vosges
17. Sacré-Coeur
18. Ste-Chapelle
M Métro Stop

2. OVERVIEW

Paris is a large metropolis, home to millions. Sure, it's a city where people live and work, but in Paris, they carry *baguettes*, stop at sidewalk cafés, and have a leisurely cup of coffee or glass of wine.

If you have only **a few days in Paris**, I'll make it easy for you to truly experience the city instead of spending your time waiting in line at museums. Helpful walks through the most interesting areas of the city are included. You'll also discover where the locals eat while avoiding tourist traps. In other words, you'll experience Paris like Parisians do.

Take great museums (like the Musée d'Orsay), amazing monuments (like the Eiffel Tower), historic churches (like Notre-Dame), fantastic neighborhoods (like the Marais) and mix with excellent French cuisine and you've got the ingredients for **great weekends in Paris**.

And if you have more time to explore this fantastic city, you'll find **three week-long plans**:

* **Museums, Art and Architecture**: The best museums, incredible art and remarkable monuments all await you in this week-long plan.

* **Eating, Drinking, Shopping and Relaxing**: This week-long plan is light on museums and heavy on experiencing incredible French cuisine and wine, checking out the great shops of Paris, and relaxing at Parisian parks and cafés.

* **Offbeat and Off the Beaten Path**: This week-long plan takes you away from the city center so that you can experience some of the neighborhoods and sights that are off the beaten path and some sights that are just, well, offbeat!

Another option is to just pick out those plans that sound interesting and make up the perfect itinerary for you.

Paris is divided into 20 arrondissements or districts, each with its own city hall, police station, post office and mayor.

Islands
The Île de la Cité is the birthplace of Paris. Surrounded by the Seine River, this island is home to Notre-Dame, Ste-Chapelle and the Conciergerie. The Île St-Louis is a charming residential island.

1st and 2nd Arrondissements
The 1st is the center of Paris where many tourist attractions are found, including the Louvre, Palais Royal and Jardin des Tuileries. The adjoining 2nd is primarily a business district.

3rd and 4th Arrondissements
The Marais is comprised of roughly the 3rd and 4th arrondissements on the Right Bank. This area, with its small streets and beautiful squares, is filled with interesting shops. It's home to both a thriving Jewish community and a large gay community. It's considered the "cœur historique," historic heart of Paris, and has retained some of the flavor of the French Renaissance.

5th and 6th Arrondissements
The 5th and 6th, south of Île de la Cité on the Left Bank of the Seine, is home to the Quartier Latin (Latin Quarter). It's a

Best Eats Details

I refer to restaurants and cafés throughout this book. For more information, see the *Best Sleeps & Eats chapter.*

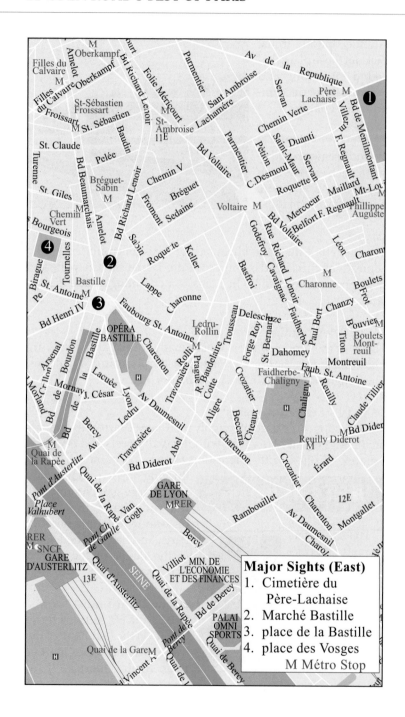

Major Sights (East)
1. Cimetière du Père-Lachaise
2. Marché Bastille
3. place de la Bastille
4. place des Vosges
M Métro Stop

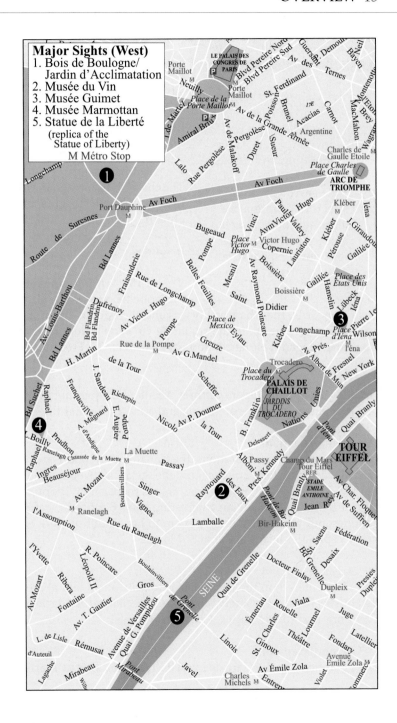

Major Sights (West)
1. Bois de Boulogne/
   Jardin d'Acclimatation
2. Musée du Vin
3. Musée Guimet
4. Musée Marmottan
5. Statue de la Liberté
   (replica of the
   Statue of Liberty)
M Métro Stop

Best Neighborhoods

- the Marais, the historic heart of Paris
- St-Germain-des-Prés, filled with upscale galleries, boutiques and restaurants
- the narrow, winding streets of Montmartre
- Montorgueil, a lively quarter where diverse shops line the pedestrian streets

maze of small streets and squares surrounding La Sorbonne, the famous university. The name Latin Quarter comes from the university tradition of speaking and studying in Latin.

7th Arrondissement

The chic 7th is home to some of the city's grandest sights, including the Eiffel Tower, Musée d'Orsay and Les Invalides.

8th and 16th Arrondissements

Luxurious shopping, the place de la Concorde, the Champs-Élysées and the Arc de Triomphe are all found in the 8th. In the adjoining 16th, you'll find upscale shopping, elegant residences and parks such as the Trocadéro.

9th Arrondissement

Home to the opulent Opéra Garnier, a center for shopping (most major department stores are here), and a mecca for nightlife.

10th Arrondissement

Home to two great train stations, the Gare du Nord and Gare de l'Est. It wasn't too long ago that guidebooks didn't even mention the 10th. Today, this working-class area is increasingly popular with artists, making for an interesting mix. Boutiques, cafés, galleries and trendy restaurants seem to have multiplied overnight, especially near the Canal St-Martin.

11th Arrondissement

The 11th, centered on the Bastille, is primarily a residential area that has become increasingly hip lately, especially around rue de Charonne and rue de Lappe. Great restaurants!

12th Arrondissement

The 12th is home to the Gare de Lyon train station. This primarily residential area is bordered on the east by the Bois de Vincennes, a beautiful park.

13th Arrondissement
The 13th is a residential area, home to Chinatown and the grand National Library.

14th and 15th Arrondissements
Known as Montparnasse and centered around the lively boulevard Montparnasse (once the center of Paris's avant-garde scene), these areas are primarily residential.

17th Arrondissement
The Arc de Triomphe and beautiful Parc Monceau border the residential 17th.

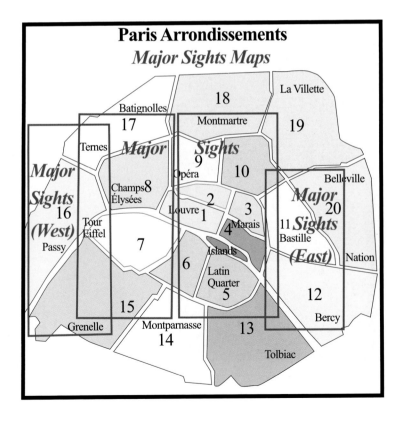

18th Arrondissement

Once a small village of vineyards and windmills, Montmartre is dominated by the massive Sacred Heart Basilica. It's also home to the sleazy place Pigalle and the largest flea market in Paris.

19th Arrondissement

Diverse residential area, home to the futuristic Parc de la Villette.

20th Arrondissement

Dominated by the Cimetière du Père-Lachaise. Another diverse neighborhood.

Finding an Address

Address numbers begin at the Seine River for north-south streets. East-west addresses run parallel to the river (following the course of the river). Street signs aren't like at home. They are at the corner of the street, but usually on a plaque attached to the building, way above eye level.

3. GREAT ONE-DAY PLANS

If you have only a day in Paris, I'll make sure you truly experience the city instead of spending your time waiting in line at museums. You'll discover where the locals eat while avoiding tourist traps. In other words, you'll experience Paris like Parisians do.

I offer two options for enjoying a full day in Paris. Both give you a few of the must-see sights and neighborhoods. I've laid each out in an easy-to-follow plan that leads from one attraction to the next. And of course, both feature what many consider the most important reason to visit Paris: incredible food and wine!

ONE GREAT DAY IN PARIS / #1

You're going to experience the wonderful city of Paris by hitting favorite sights, with a schedule that's not too hectic and overwhelming. With only a day, see **Notre-Dame** and the **Eiffel Tower**. Even though the huge Louvre is the greatest art museum in the world, don't try to conquer it at the expense of seeing the rest of Paris. I'll just take you to see the fantastic **glass-pyramid entrance**. And since a highlight (if not *the* highlight) of any day in Paris is experiencing **fabulous French cuisine**, I've recommended a few great restaurants.

You'll start your day at any typical Parisian café near your hotel. Why don't you start by having coffee and a *croissant*? If you order *un café*, you'll get a small cup of very strong black coffee. If you'd like a larger cup of coffee with steamed milk, ask for *un crème*. For the cost of a cup of coffee, you can linger at a café and watch the world pass you by for as long as you want. It's one of Paris's greatest bargains.

After you've had your Parisian coffee, jump on the métro to our first sight. One way to experience the islands in the middle of the Seine River is to take the **Islands Walk** in the *Walks* chapter of this book. The highlights of this walk include **Notre-Dame**, **Ste-Chapelle** and **Île St-Louis**.

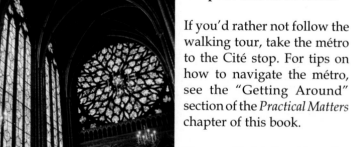

If you'd rather not follow the walking tour, take the métro to the Cité stop. For tips on how to navigate the métro, see the "Getting Around" section of the *Practical Matters* chapter of this book.

First you'll visit **Ste-Chapelle**. On a sunny day, you'll be

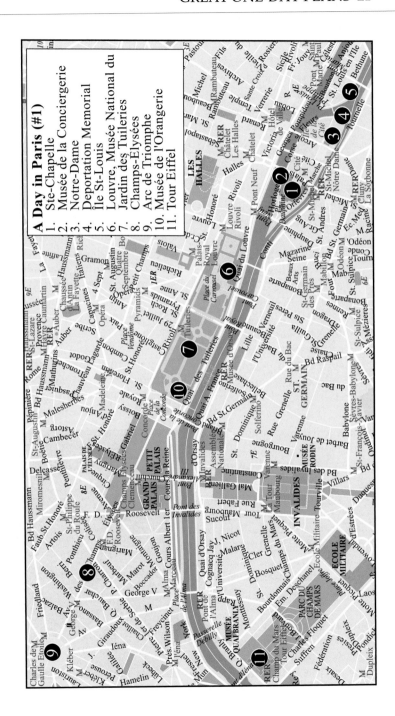

A Day in Paris (#1)
1. Ste-Chapelle
2. Musée de la Conciergerie
3. Notre-Dame
4. Deportation Memorial
5. Île St-Louis
6. Louvre, Musée National du
7. Jardin des Tuileries
8. Champs-Elysées
9. Arc de Triomphe
10. Musée de l'Orangerie
11. Tour Eiffel

dazzled by nearly 6,600 square feet of stained glass at this Gothic masterpiece. Fifteen windows depict biblical scenes from the Garden of Eden to the Apocalypse (the large rose window). Built in 1246, it took less than two years to build, an amazing feat when one realizes that Notre-Dame took over two centuries to complete. *Info*: 1st/Métro Cité. 4 boulevard du Palais. Tel. 01/53.40.60.80. Open daily Mar-Oct 9:30am-6pm, Nov-Feb 9am-5pm. Closed Jan 1, May 1 and Dec 25. Admission: €7 adults, €4 ages 18-25, under 18 free.

On the same island is the **Cathédrale Notre-Dame**, one of the greatest achievements of Gothic architecture. It's so huge that it can accommodate over 6,000 visitors. The interior is dominated by three beautiful (and immense) rose windows, and has a 7,800-pipe organ. Inside along the walls are individual chapels dedicated to saints. The most famous chapel is that of Joan of Arc in the right transept. The treasury houses relics, manuscripts and religious garments.

You may want to climb the 387 steps of the north tower for a grand view of Paris. You'll also have a great view of the cathedral's famous

gargoyles. *Info*: 4th/Métro Cité. 6 place du Parvis Notre-Dame. Tel. 01/42.34.56.10. Open daily 8am-6:45pm. Tower open daily Apr-June and Sep 9:30am-7:30pm, Jul and Aug 9am-7:30pm, Oct-Mar 10am-5:30pm. Admission: Free to the cathedral. Towers: €6, under 18 free. Treasury: €6.

After visiting these two churches, make sure you head to an overlooked sight directly behind the cathedral. Cross the street (quai Archevêché) and head through the gate.

It will take you only a short time to walk through the **Mémorial des Martyrs Français de la Déportation de 1945** (Deportation Memorial). This free memorial was built in honor of the more than 30,000 citizens who were placed on boats at this spot for deportation to concentration camps. You descend steps and become surrounded by walls. Don't miss this memorial. It's both moving and disturbing.

When you leave the Deportation Memorial, head to the pedestrian bridge.

The bridge **Pont St-Louis** takes you to the **Île St-Louis**, a residential island within the city. The vast majority of the buildings on this island date back to the 1600s, making for a beauti- ful place to stroll, especially the small side streets. There are interesting shops and several good restaurants.

After you cross the bridge you'll be on the narrow **rue St-Louis-en-l'Île**, one of the most beautiful streets in all of Paris. The highlight of this street is at number 31. Tour- ists and Parisians alike line up at the carry-out window of **Berthillon** for the best- known ice cream in Paris.

Over thirty flavors from *chocolat blanc* (white chocolate) to *pain d'épice* (gingerbread). Closed Mon, Tue and Aug. Can you believe that an ice-cream shop is closed during the hottest month of the year?

If you're up for more sights, walk to or navigate the métro to the Palais Royal stop. From here, you'll head into the courtyard of the Louvre.

ALTERNATIVE PLAN
If you're determined to see at least some of the **Louvre**, check out the tour of the **Denon Wing** on Saturday of Weekend #3 of this book. Highlights include the *Mona Lisa* and *Vénus de Milo*.

Simply put, the **Louvre** is the greatest art museum in the world. But if you have only a short stay in Paris, don't try to conquer it at the expense of seeing the rest of Paris. It's huge. It's the largest art museum in the world, the largest building in Paris, and it's in the largest palace in Europe.

The inner courtyard of the Louvre is the site of the fantastic **glass pyramid**, designed by the famous architect I.M. Pei, that serves as the main entrance to the museum. The popular **Café Marly** overlooks the pyramid and is a good place for lunch or a drink. *Info*: 1st/ Métro Musée du Louvre/ Palais-Royal. 93 rue de Rivoli. Tel. 01/49.26.06.60. Open daily 8am to 2am. Another choice nearby is **Muscade** in the lovely and tranquil gardens of the

nearby Palais Royal. This little restaurant/tea room serves great salads and delicious homemade desserts. *Info*: 1st/Métro Palais Royal. 36 rue de Montpensier (within the Palais Royal gardens). Tel. 01/42.97.51.36. Dinner served from May to Aug. www.muscade-palais-royal.com.

After you've taken photos of the glass pyramid, head in the opposite direction of the Louvre (west) and into the gardens.

The **Jardin des Tuileries** takes its name from the word *tuil* or tile (roof-tile factories once were here). You'll enjoy bubbling fountains, statues, flowers and trees between the Louvre and place de la Concorde. Sit down and relax in this beautiful garden in the middle of Paris. You can catch a glimpse of the Eiffel Tower from here. There are also several cafés in the garden.

At the west end of the gardens, at the **place de la Concorde**, you can look down the **Champs-Élysées** to the **Arc de Triomphe**.

If you have the time, you should visit the **Musée de l'Orangerie**. This former 19th-century greenhouse is situated at the west end of the Tuileries garden. It's home to a collection of paintings from the late 19th century and the first half of the 20th century (including 15 Cézannes, 24 Renoirs, 10 Matisses and 12 Picassos). Of particular note are the large *Water Lilies* by **Monet**. While visiting the Louvre can be overwhelming (so many paintings, so little time), the Orangerie is small and manageable. After years of renovation, it's finally  reopened and it's magnificent. Note that if you're not a member of a group with reservations, the museum isn't open to individual visitors until 12:30pm. *Info*: 1st/Métro Concorde. 1 place de la Concorde. Tel. 01/44.77.80.07. Open Wed-Mon 9am-12:30pm (groups), 12:30pm-7pm (Fri until 9pm) (individuals). Closed Tue. Admission: €7, under 18 free. Free on the first Sun of each month.

A highlight (if not *the* highlight) of any day in Paris is dining. It's hard to have a bad meal in Paris. For dinner choose either **La Fontaine de Mars** (*Info*: 7th/Métro École Militaire. 129 rue St-

Dominique. Tel. 01/47.05.46.44. Moderate) or **Restaurant de la Tour** (*Info*: 15th/Métro Dupleix. 6 rue Desaix. Tel. 01/43.06.04.24. Closed Sun and Mon. Moderate). Both are wonderful French dining experiences.

After dinner visit the **Eiffel Tower** (both restaurants are near it). The lines will be short, the view memorable, and the light show on the hour is spectacular (the tower's lights glitter for ten minutes on the hour). There's no better way to end your day! *Info*: 7th/Métro Trocadéro, École Militaire or Bir-Hakeim. Champ-de-Mars. Tel. 01/44.11.23.23. Open daily. Elevator: Jan-Jun 15 and Sep-Dec 9:30am-11:45pm. Final ascension 11pm (10:30pm for top floor), Jun 16-Aug 9am-12:45pm. Final ascension midnight (11pm for top floor). Stairs (first and second floors): Jan-Jun 15 and Sep-

Dec 9:30am-6:30pm (final admittance 6pm), Jun 16-Aug 9am-12:30am (final admittance midnight). Admission: To the first landing €4.20, second landing €7.70 and third landing €11. Stairs to the second floor €3.80, €3 under 25. www.toureiffel.fr.

ONE GREAT DAY IN PARIS / #2

As an alternative to the first day plan set out in this chapter, we'll spend more time at the **Eiffel Tower** and make it our first stop. Then off to the **Marais** neighborhood and one of Paris's premier sights, the stunning **place des Vosges**. On the way here, and later today, we can admire some spectacular architecture, maybe check out another museum or two, and end the day with a great dinner and a walk along the banks of the **Seine**.

As in the first day plan earlier in this chapter, my advice is the same: start your day at a Parisian café with coffee and a *croissant*. Then get on the métro to our first sight. For tips on how to navigate the métro, see the "Getting Around" section in the *Practical Matters* chapter of this book.

An easy way to see many sights in one day is to take the **Major Sights Walk** in the *Walks* chapter of this book. It begins at the École Militaire métro stop. Highlights include the **Tour Eiffel** (Eiffel Tower), **Arc de Triomphe**, and **Champs-Élysées**.

If you're not interested in taking the walk, take the métro to the École Militaire stop and follow the plan below.

Constructed in 1889, the **Tour Eiffel** (Eiffel Tower) was called, among other things, an "iron monster" when it was erected. Gustave-Alexandre Eiffel never meant for his 7,000-ton tower to be permanent, and it was almost torn down in 1909. French radio, however, needing a broadcast tower, saved it from destruction. Today, it's without a doubt the most recognizable structure in the world. You can either take the elevator to one of three landings or climb the 1,652 stairs. You cannot visit Paris without a trip to this wonderful structure. *Info*: 7th/Métro Trocadéro, École Militaire or Bir-Hakeim. Champ-de-Mars. Tel. 01/44.11.23.23. Open daily. Elevator: Jan-Jun 15 and Sep-Dec 9:30am-11:45pm. Final ascension 11pm (10:30pm for top floor), Jun 16-Aug 9am-12:45pm.

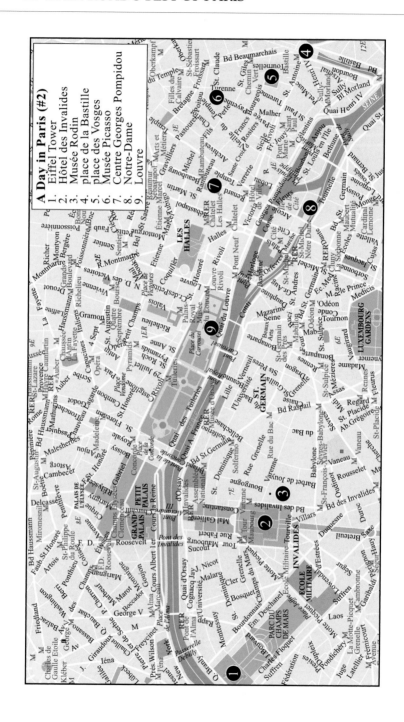

A Day in Paris (#2)
1. Eiffel Tower
2. Hôtel des Invalides
3. Musée Rodin
4. place de la Bastille
5. place des Vosges
6. Musée Picasso
7. Centre Georges Pompidou
8. Notre-Dame
9. Louvre

Final ascension midnight (11pm for top floor). Stairs (first and second floors): Jan-Jun 15 and Sep-Dec 9:30am-6:30pm (final admittance 6pm), Jun 16-Aug 9am-12:30am (final admittance midnight). Admission: To the first landing €4.20, second landing €7.70 and third landing €11. Stairs to the second floor €3.80, €3 under 25. www.toureiffel.fr.

Nearby is the **Hôtel des Invalides**, built in 1670 for disabled soldiers. The world's greatest military museum, **Musée de l'Armée** (Army Museum), is here, as is the second-tallest monument in Paris, the **Eglise du Dôme** (Dome Church). The main attraction here is **Napoléon's Tomb**, an enormous red stone sarcophagus. For such a tiny man, everything here is huge. *Info*: 7th/Métro Invalides or La Tour-Maubourg. 129 rue de Grenelle. Tel. 01/44.42.38.77. Open daily Oct-Mar 10am-5pm, Apr-Sep 10am-6pm. Closed first Mon of each month and Jan 1, May 1, Nov 1, Dec 25. Admission: €8, under 18 free. www.invalides.org.

Now, head to the **place de la Bastille**. There are plenty of cafés here. The notorious Bastille prison was torn down over 200 years ago by mobs during the French Revolution. Today, it's a roundabout traffic circle where cars speed around the 170-foot **Colonne de Jullet** (July Column). On the opposite side is the modern **Opéra Bastille**.

Head down rue St-Antoine (in the opposite direction of the Opéra Bastille). You're now in the **Marais**. This area, with its small streets and beautiful squares, is filled with interesting shops. It's considered the "cœur historique," historic heart of Paris, and has retained some of the flavor of the French Renaissance. To truly experience Paris like the Parisians do, take a stroll through this great neighborhood. Sit at a

ALTERNATIVE PLAN
If you're not a history buff, visit the nearby Musée Rodin (Rodin Museum). This museum is in Rodin's former studio, an 18th-century mansion with a beautiful rose garden. His best-known work, *The Thinker*, is here. *Info*: 7th/Métro Varenne. 77 rue de Varenne. Tel. 01/44.18.61.10. Open Tue-Sun Apr-Sep 9:30am-5:45pm, Oct-Mar 9:30am-4:45pm. Closed Mon. Admission: €6, under 18 free. €1 (garden only). www.musee-rodin.fr.

café, window-shop or just take in the beauty of this fabulous city. The highlight is the **place des Vosges**, the oldest square in the city

(enter from rue de Birague off of rue St-Antoine). It's simply the most beautiful square in Paris, in France, and probably in all of Europe. Don't miss it!

Need a break? Stop at **Ma Bourgogne**. This café/restaurant on the square serves traditional Parisian cuisine and specializes in roast chicken. *Info*: 19 place des Vosges. Tel. 01/42.78.44.64. No credit cards. Moderate.

If you're interested in visiting a museum, here are two choices:

The **Musée Picasso** has the largest Picasso collection in the world (not to mention works by Renoir, Cézanne, Degas and Matisse). *Info*: 3rd/Métro St-Sébastien or St-Paul. 5 rue de Thorigny. Tel. 01/42.71.25.21. Open Apr-Sep 9:30am-6pm, Oct-Mar 9:30am-5:30pm. Closed Tue. Admission: €9.50, €7.50 ages 18-25, under 18 free. Free the first Sun of the month. www.musee-picasso.fr.

The **Centre Georges Pompidou** houses an incredible collection of contemporary art. The building is a work of art in itself. It's "ekoskeletal" (all the plumbing, elevators, and ducts are exposed and brightly painted). This museum has works by Picasso, Matisse, Kandinsky, Pollock, and many other favorite modern artists. *Info*: 4th/Métro Rambuteau. place Georges-Pompidou (on rue St-Martin between rue Rambuteau and rue St-Merri). Tel. 01/44.78.12.33. Open Wed-Mon 11am-10pm. Closed Tue and May 1. Admission: To the Center: €10, under 18 free. Free on the first Sun of the month. www.cnac-gp.fr.

Duck into any one of the **Nicolas** wine shops scattered throughout the city. You'll find a great selection of inexpensive (or expensive) French wines to choose to take back to your hotel and enjoy before dinner.

Best Monuments

- the **Eiffel Tower**, the most recognizable structure in the world
- the **Obelisk of Luxor**, an Egyptian column from the 13th century at the place de la Concorde
- the **Arc de Triomphe**, the largest triumphal arc in the world

For dinner, try either **Gaspard de la Nuit** (*Info*: 4th/Métro Bastille. 6 rue des Tournelles. Tel. 01/42.77.90.53. Moderate-Expensive) or **Bistrot de l'Oulette** (*Info*: 4th/Métro Bastille. 38 rue des Tournelles. Tel. 01/42.71.43.33. Closed Sat [lunch] & Sun. Moderate). Both cozy bistros are on the same street near the place des Vosges. After dinner, visit **Le Trésor** where cocktails are served both inside and outside at tables along a lovely, flowered street in the heart of the Marais. Great people-watching. *Info:* 4th/Métro Hôtel de Ville or Saint-Paul. 5-7 rue du Trésor (off of rue Vieille du Temple). Tel. 01/42.71.35.17.

End your day by heading to the **Seine River**. Walk along the river, taking in the elegantly lit **Notre-Dame** and the stunning beauty of this amazing city. If you're ambitious, you can walk all the way to the courtyard of the **Louvre** to see the lovely lit glass pyramid.

4. FANTASTIC WEEKEND PLANS

Take **great museums** (like the Musée d'Orsay and the Orangerie), **amazing monuments** (like the Eiffel Tower), **historic churches** (like Notre-Dame and Ste-Chapelle), **fantastic neighborhoods** (like the Marais and Île St-Louis) and mix with **excellent French cuisine** – and you've got the ingredients for great weekends in Paris.

I've laid out three weekend plans, plus some alternatives, each with its own map to guide you through the beautiful streets of Paris.

WEEKEND IN PARIS / #1

Friday Evening
A great way to begin your weekend in Paris is to dine at an authentic Paris eatery. On the Left Bank, try the tiny **Le Timbre** for a true Paris bistro experience. *Info*: 6th/Métro Notre-Dame-des-Champs. 3 rue Ste-Beuve (off of rue Notre-Dame-des-Champs). Closed Sun & part of Aug. Tel. 01/45.49.10.40. Inexpensive-Moderate.

On the Right Bank, try **Spicy**. This restaurant has an excellent location near the Champs-Élysées. Modern French cuisine is served by a friendly, English-speaking staff to an international clientele. *Info*: 8th/Métro F.D.-Roosevelt. 8 ave. F.D.-Roosevelt. Tel. 01/56.59.62.59. Open daily for lunch and dinner. www.spicyrestaurant.com. Moderate-Expensive.

After dinner, head to **Café Marly** at 93 rue de Rivoli (1st/Métro Palais Royal-Musée d'Orsay). You'll pay for the view overlooking the glass-pyramid entrance to the Louvre, but it's a great place to end your first day in Paris with a glass of champagne. How French! *Info*: 93 rue de Rivoli. Tel. 01/49.26.06.60. Open daily 8am to 2am.

Saturday
Start your day at the centrally located **La Ferme** at 55-57 rue St-Roch. It's a good place to relax with a great cup of coffee and have breakfast. *Info*: 1st/Métro Opéra or Pyramides. Tel. 01/40.20.12.12.

Now that you've fueled up, see the islands of Paris (including visits to **Notre-Dame** and the **Deportation Memorial**) by taking the **Islands Walk** in this book. If you'd rather not take the walk, take the métro to the Cité stop.

Don't Miss ...

- drinking champagne while looking at the glass pyramid at the Louvre
- touring the islands in the middle of the Seine River
- visiting the Arc de Triomphe and strolling down the Champs-Élysées
- wonderful French cuisine

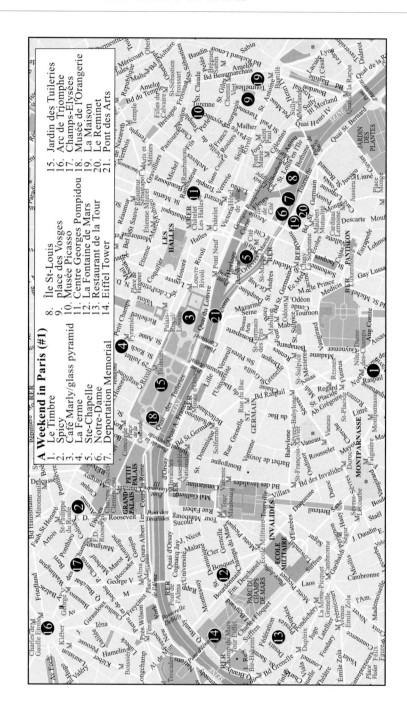

A Weekend in Paris (#1)

1. Le Timbre
2. Spicy
3. Café Marly/glass pyramid
4. La Ferme
5. Ste-Chapelle
6. Notre-Dame
7. Deportation Memorial
8. Île St-Louis
9. place des Vosges
10. Musée Picasso
11. Centre Georges Pompidou
12. La Fontaine de Mars
13. Restaurant de la Tour
14. Eiffel Tower
15. Jardin des Tuileries
16. Arc de Triomphe
17. Champs-Elysées
18. Musée de l'Orangerie
19. La Maison
20. Le Reminet
21. Pont des Arts

You'll start your sightseeing by visiting **Ste-Chapelle**. On a sunny day, you'll be dazzled by nearly 6,600 square feet of stained glass at this Gothic masterpiece. Fifteen windows depict biblical scenes from the Garden of Eden to the Apocalypse (the large rose window). Built in 1246, it took less than two years to build, an amazing feat when one realizes that Notre-Dame took over two centuries to complete. *Info*: 1st/Métro Cité. 4 boulevard du Palais. Tel. 01/53.40.60.80. Open daily Mar-Oct 9:30am-6pm, Nov-Feb 9am-5pm. Closed Jan 1, May 1 and Dec 25. Admission: €7 adults, €4 ages 18-25, under 18 free.

From here, you can head to the square in front of Notre-Dame. The **place du Parvis Notre-Dame** (recently renamed Parvis Notre-Dame/Place Jean-Paul-II) is the center of all of France. A copper plaque on the ground outside the cathedral is **Point Zéro** from which all distances in France are measured. Tradition holds that you'll be granted a wish if you stand on this point, close your eyes and turn three times. Oh, go ahead and do it!

Now we'll visit **Notre-Dame**, one of the greatest achievements of Gothic architecture. It took nearly 200 years to complete the cathedral. It's so huge that it can accommodate over 6,000 visitors. On your right when you're facing the church is the statue of Charlemagne ("Charles the Great"). On the left doorway is St. Denis holding his head. He was the first martyr of France, decapitated by a jealous king for preaching Christianity. In the center is Christ sitting on the Throne of Judgment with those damned to hell on the right in chains and those destined for heaven on the left.

The interior is dominated by three beautiful (and huge) rose windows, and has a 7,800-pipe organ. Inside along the walls are individual chapels dedicated to saints. The most famous chapel is that of Joan of Arc in the right transept. The sacristy houses relics, manuscripts and religious garments.

If you're afraid of heights or just don't want to climb the tower, make sure you take a look at the sides of the church. You'll see the "flying buttresses" (50-foot beams that support the Gothic structure).

But if you decide to climb the 387 steps of the north tower, you'll have a grand view of Paris. You'll also have a great view of the cathedral's famous gargoyles. *Info*: 4th/Métro Cité. 6 place du Parvis Notre-Dame. Tel. 01/42.34.56.10. Open daily 8am-6:45pm. Tower open daily Apr-June and Sep 9:30am-7:30pm, Jul and Aug 9am-7:30pm, Oct-Mar 10am-5:30pm. Admission: Free to the cathedral. Towers: €6, under 18 free. Treasury: €6.

Behind the cathedral is the **Mémorial des Martyrs Français de la Déportation de 1945** (Deportation Memorial). This free memorial was built in honor of the more than 30,000 citizens who were placed on boats at this spot for deportation to concentration camps. You descend steps and become surrounded by walls. The plaque on the floor reads: "They descended into the mouth of the earth and they did not return." A hallway is covered with 200,000 lit crystals (one for each French citizen who died). At the far end of the hall is the eternal flame of hope. Don't miss this memorial. It's both moving and disturbing. *Info*: 4th/Métro Cité. Open daily 10am-noon and 2pm to 5pm (until 7pm in summer). Admission: Free.

You can cross the bridge behind Notre-Dame to the **Île St-Louis**, a residential island within the city. The vast majority of the buildings on this island date back to the 1600s, making for a beautiful place to stroll, especially the small side streets. There are interesting shops and several good restaurants.

Now, take the métro to the St-Paul stop and the Marais. The Marais neighborhood, with its small streets and beautiful squares, is filled with interesting shops and plenty of places for lunch. It's considered the historic heart of Paris. To experience it, take the **Marais Walk** in this book. At the end of the walk, you'll visit the **Café Beaubourg** facing the Pompidou Center. Great people-watching!

If you'd rather not take the walk, head to the St-Paul métro and walk east on rue St-Antoine (on the left side of the street) until you reach rue de Birague. Turn left and then head to the beautiful **place des Vosges**. It's not only the oldest square in the city, but it's also the most beautiful square in Paris, in France, and probably in all of Europe. The area around the square is a wonderful place to stroll and take in the beauty of this fabulous city. The Marais is a shopper's paradise with unique boutiques from kitschy to upscale, especially on and around the rue des Francs-Bourgeois. There are plenty of places to take a break and have a drink or snack.

If you're interested in visiting a museum, there are several famous ones in the Marais.

The **Musée Picasso** has the largest Picasso collection in the world (not to mention works by Renoir, Cézanne, Degas and Matisse). *Info*: 3rd/Métro St-Sébastien or St-Paul. 5 rue de Thorigny. Tel. 01/ 42.71.25.21. Open Apr-Sep 9:30am-6pm, Oct-Mar 9:30am-5:30pm. Closed Tue. Admission: €9.50, €7.50 ages 18-25, under 18 free. Free the first Sun of the month. www.musee-picasso.fr.

The **Centre Georges Pompidou** houses an incredible collection of 20th- and 21st-century art. The building is a work of art in itself. Opened in 1977, the controversial building is "ekoskeletal" (all the plumbing, elevators, and ducts are exposed and brightly painted). *Info*: 4th/Métro Rambuteau. place Georges-Pompidou (on rue St-Martin between rue Rambuteau and rue St-Merri). Tel. 01/44.78.12.33. Open Wed-Mon 11am-10pm. Closed Tue and May 1. Admission: To the Center: €10, under 18 free. Free on the first Sun of the month. www.cnac-gp.fr.

For dinner choose either **La Fontaine de Mars** (*Info*: 7th/Métro École Militaire. 129 rue St-Dominique. Tel. 01/47.05.46.44. Moderate) or **Restaurant de la Tour** (*Info*: 15th/Métro Dupleix. 6 rue

Desaix. Tel. 01/43.06.04.24. Closed Sun and Mon. Moderate). Both are wonderful French dining experiences.

After dinner visit the **Eiffel Tower** (both restaurants are near it). The lines will be short, the view memorable, and the light show on the hour is spectacular. There's no better way to end your day! *Info*: 7th/Métro Trocadéro, École Militaire or Bir-Hakeim. Champ de Mars. Tel. 01/44.11.23.23. Open daily. Elevator: Jan-Jun 15 and Sep-Dec 9:30am-11:45pm. Final ascension 11pm (10:30pm for top floor), Jun 16-Aug 9am-12:45pm. Final ascension midnight (11pm for top floor). Stairs (first and second floors): Jan-Jun 15 and Sep-Dec 9:30am-6:30pm (final admittance 6pm), Jun 16-Aug 9am-12:30am (final admittance midnight). Admission: To the first landing €4.20, second landing €7.70 and third landing €11. Stairs to the second floor €3.80, €3 under 25. www.toureiffel.fr.

Sunday

Start your day in the lovely **Jardin des Tuileries**. While in the park, stop at **Café Very**, for a *croissant* and cup of coffee.

A great way to see lots of sights (including the **Arc de Triomphe** and the **Champs-Élysées**) is to take the **Major Sights Walk** in this book. There are plenty of places to relax along the walk.

If you're not interested in taking the Major Sights Walk, take the métro to the Charles-de-Gaulle-Étoile stop. You'll be at the **Arc de Triomphe**.

Don't try to walk across the square. This is Paris's busiest intersection. Twelve streets pour into the circle around the Arc. Instead, there are underground passages that will take you here. It's the largest triumphal arch in the world. Napoléon commissioned it in 1806 and it was completed in 1836. The Arc is the home to the

Tomb of the Unknown Soldier, and is engraved with the names of generals in Napoléon's victories.

There's an observation deck providing one of the greatest views of Paris. There's no cost to visit the Arc, but there's an admission fee for the exhibit of photos of the Arc throughout history and for the observation deck. If you aren't impressed by the view down the **Champs-Élysées**, you really shouldn't have come to Paris. *Info*: 8th/Métro Charles-de-Gaulle-Étoile. place Charles-de-Gaulle-Étoile. Tel. 01/55.37.73.77. Open daily Apr-Sep 10am-11pm, Oct-Mar 10:30am-10:30pm. Admission: €8, under 18 free.

After you've visited the Arc de Triomphe walk down the **Champs-Élysées**, one of the most famous streets in the world. At the end of the street, you'll find yourself at the **place de la Concorde**. In the center stands the **Obelisk of Luxor**, an Egyptian column from the 13th century covered with hieroglyphics. On the other side of the square is the **Jardin des Tuileries** (where you started your day). Head to the **Musée de l'Orangerie**. This former 19th-century  greenhouse is situated in the beautiful Tuileries garden. It's home to a collection of paintings from the late 19th century and the first half of the 20th century (including 15 Cézannes, 24 Renoirs, 10 Matisses and 12 Picassos).

Of particular note are *Les Grandes Décorations*, Japanese-inspired paintings of water-lily gardens. These 22 six-foot-high canvases are stunningly displayed in two oval-shaped white rooms. While visiting the Louvre can be overwhelming (so many paintings, so little time), the Orangerie is small and manageable. After years of renovation, it's finally reopened and it's magnificent. Note that if you're not a member of a group with reservations, the museum isn't open to individual visitors until 12:30pm. *Info*: 1st/Métro

Concorde. 1 place de la Concorde. Tel. 01/44.77.80.07. Open Wed-Mon 9am-12:30pm (groups), 12:30pm-7pm (Fri until 9pm) (individuals). Closed Tue. Admission: €7, under 18 free. Free on the first Sun of each month.

After visiting the museum, make sure to stop into any one of the **Nicolas** wine shops scattered throughout the city, where you'll find a great selection of inexpensive French wines. (You can also find inexpensive and decent French wines at neighborhood grocery stores.)

For dinner, try the fun **La Maison** (*Info*: 5th/Métro St-Michel. 1 rue de la Bûcherie. Tel. 01/43.29.73.57. Closed Mon. Moderate) or the nearby **Le Reminet**, a small Latin Quarter bistro with modern French cooking. *Info*: 5th/Métro Maubert-Mutualité. 5 rue des Grands-Degrés. Tel. 01/44.07.04.24. Closed Tue, Wed & part of Aug. Moderate.

After dinner, head to the Seine River. There are 36 bridges over the Seine that don't just connect one bank with the other, they should be considered monuments in and of themselves. They are places for strolling, for stopping to kiss someone you love, for viewing the beauty of Paris and pondering life. A favorite is the **Pont des Arts**, at the tip of the Île de la Cité. It dates back to 1803 and was the first pedestrian-only bridge in Paris. It has a fantastic view of the Pont Neuf, the Louvre and Notre-Dame. (Métro Louvre). What a way to end your weekend!

WEEKEND IN PARIS / #2

Friday Evening
A good choice for dinner on your first night is **Le Reminet**, a small Latin Quarter bistro with modern French cooking. The French love to have an *apéritif*, a drink before dinner. Why not order a glass of champagne or have a delicious (and oh so French) *kir royal*, champagne with *crème de cassis* (black currant liqueur), while you look over the menu? *Info*: 5th/Métro Maubert-Mutualité. 5 rue des Grands-Degrés. Tel. 01/44.07.04.24. Closed Tue, Wed & part of Aug. Moderate.

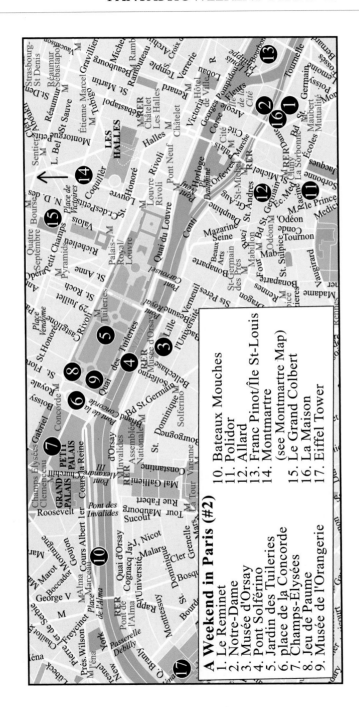

A Weekend in Paris (#2)

1. Le Reminet
2. Notre-Dame
3. Musée d'Orsay
4. Pont Solférino
5. Jardin des Tuileries
6. place de la Concorde
7. Champs-Élysées
8. Jeu de Paume
9. Musée de l'Orangerie
10. Bateaux Mouches
11. Polidor
12. Allard
13. Franc Pinot/Île St-Louis
14. Montmartre
    (see Montmartre Map)
15. Le Grand Colbert
16. La Maison
17. Eiffel Tower

Don't Miss ...

- Impressionist art at the Musée d'Orsay
- relaxing in the Jardin des Tuileries
- a boat tour on the Seine River
- exploring Montmartre

Le Reminet is on the Left Bank, just south of the Seine River and Notre-Dame. So, after dinner, head to **Notre-Dame** and stroll along the islands in the middle of Paris.

Saturday
Start you day with a visit to the **Musée d'Orsay**, a magnificent museum. Get there early to avoid the lines, and after you've entered the museum, go to the **Café des Hauteurs** on the 5th floor. The café opens at 10:30am.

The **Musée d'Orsay** is located across the Seine from the Tuileries and the Louvre in a former train station that has been gloriously converted into 80 galleries. Many of the most famous Impressionist and Post-Impressionist works are here. Some of the paintings here are:

- Whistler's *Whistler's Mother*
- Manet's *Olympia* and *Picnic on the Grass*
- Dega's *Absinthe*
- Renoir's *Moulin de la Galette*
- Monet's *Magpie*

There are also works by Sargent, Pissaro and van Gogh, just to name a few. *Info*: 7th/Métro Solférino. 1 rue de la Légion d'Honneur. Tel. 01/40.49.48.14. Open Tue-Sun 9:30am-6pm (Thu until 9:45pm. Closed Mon, Jan 1, May 1 and Dec 25. Admission: €7.50, €5.50 ages 18-25, under 18 free. €5.50 on Sun and after 4:15pm (after 8pm on Thu). Additional €1.50 for special exhibits. www.musee-orsay.fr.

You can have a reasonably priced buffet lunch in an ornate dining room at the museum at the **Restaurant du Musée d'Orsay**. *Info*: Tel. 01/45.49.47.03. Lunch 11:45am to 2:45 pm. Dinner Thu only 7pm to 9:30pm. Closed Mon.

Not interested in dining at a museum? Try the delicious roasted chicken at **Les Deux Musées** just down the street from the Musée d'Orsay. *Info*: 7th/Métro Solférino. 5 rue Bellechasse. Tel. 01/45.55.13.39.

After lunch, head to the Seine River and the **Pont Solférino**. This double-decker bridge spans the Seine near the Musée d'Orsay. It's located at one of the most beautiful spots along the river. (Métro Solférino)

If you walk on the lower level of the bridge, continue under the street on the other side and you'll be in the lovely **Jardin des Tuileries**. The same man who planned the gardens of Versailles designed the Tuileries. The garden takes its name from the word *tuil* or tile (roof-tile factories once were here). You'll enjoy bubbling fountains, statues, flowers and trees between the Louvre and place de la Concorde. Sit down and relax in this beautiful garden in the middle of Paris. *Info*: 1st/Métro Tuileries or Concorde. West of the Louvre to the place de la Concorde.

From here, you can either call it a day or head west through the gardens to the **place de la Concorde**. This square is huge (21 acres) and in the center stands the **Obelisk of Luxor**, an Egyptian column from the 13th century covered with hieroglyphics. It was moved here in 1833. Now a traffic roundabout, it was here that King Louis XVI and Marie-Antoinette were guillotined during the French Revolution. The name is ironic as *concorde* means "harmony." *Info*: 8th/Métro Concorde. Between the Jardin des Tuileries and the Champs-Élysées.

Off of this square is the **Avenue des Champs-Élysées**, one of the most famous streets in the world. It's the site of the victory parade of the Allies in World War II, the annual military parade every July 14, and the final leg of the Tour de France bicycle race. The Champs-Élysées is home to expensive retail shops, fast-food

chains, car dealers, banks, huge movie theatres and overpriced cafés. Despite this, you can sit at a café and experience great people-watching (mostly tourists, but one of the most diverse groups of people you'll ever see). At the far west end is the **Arc de Triomphe**.

If you're interested in photography, you can visit the **Galerie Nationale du Jeu de Paume** in the northeast corner of the Jardin des Tuileries. Named after a ball game similar to tennis that was played here, this museum houses the national video and photography museum. *Info*: 1st/Métro Concorde. Northeast corner of the Jardin des Tuileries at 1 place de la Concorde. Tel. 01/47.03.12.50. Open Tue noon-9pm, Wed-Fri noon-7pm, Sat-Sun 10am-7pm. Closed Mon. Admission: €6, under 13 free. www.jeudepaume.org.

Also here is the **Musée de l'Orangerie**. This former 19th-century greenhouse is home to a collection of paintings from the late 19th century and the first half of the 20th century (including 15 Cézannes, 24 Renoirs, 10 Matisses and 12 Picassos). Of particular note are the eight large *Water Lilies* that Monet gave France in 1922. After years of renovation, it's finally reopened and it's magnificent. Note that if you're not a member of a group with reservations, the museum isn't open to individual visitors until 12:30pm. *Info*: 1st/Métro Concorde. 1 place de la Concorde. Tel. 01/44.77.80.07. Open Wed-Mon 9am-12:30pm (groups), 12:30pm-7pm (Fri until

9pm) (individuals). Closed Tue. Admission: €7, under 18 free. Free on the first Sun of each month.

For dinner, you have two very different choices. If you're visiting Paris for the first time, a good way to tour the Seine River and get a good overview of Paris is on the **Bateaux-Mouches** boat tour. The boats depart regularly from the Right Bank next to the place de l'Alma (near the Eiffel Tower). (Métro Alma-Marceau). Dinner  cruises cost €125 (cheaper if you're a member of a group). Lunch cruises cost €50. Reservations are essential. *Info*: Tel. 01/42.25.96.10, www.bateauxmouches.com). A 75-minute day cruise costs about €8.

If a boat tour is just not your style, head to the Left Bank for dinner at either **Polidor**, a popular 1930s bistro serving traditional Parisian cuisine (*Info*: 6th/Métro Odéon. 41 rue Monsieur-le-Prince. Tel. 01/43.26.95.34. No reservations. No credit cards. Inexpensive) or **Allard**, where diners repeatedly praise the food at this typical Parisian bistro. (*Info*: 6th/Métro Odéon. 41 rue St-André-des-Arts. Tel. 01/43.26.48.23. Closed Sun & part of Aug. Moderate).

If you're up for more (you're on vacation after all), you can end your evening at **Franc Pinot**, an intimate jazz club at 1 quai de Bourbon on the Île St-Louis. If you're not into jazz, just wander the quiet streets of the charming **Île St-Louis**. *Info*: 4th/Métro Pont Marie. Tel 01/46.33.60.64.

Sunday
Discover the Montmartre neighborhood by taking the **Montmartre Walk** in this book. Highlights include **Sacré-Coeur**, **Espace Salvador Dali**, and the **Moulin Rouge**.

If you're not up to the walk, take the métro to the Abbesses stop to see the **Basilique du Sacré-Coeur** (Sacred Heart Basilica).

To avoid climbing the hundreds of steps to the basilica, you can take the métro to Abbesses, then take the elevator and follow the signs to the funicular (cable car), which will take you up to the Basilica for the price of a métro ticket. (A fun curiosity just behind the Métro Abbesses is the "Love Wall" where "I love you" is written in what looks like a zillion languages.)

You could also head directly up **Rue Foyatier**. With over 200 steps, this "street" is west (left) of the hill leading up to Sacré-Coeur. It's one of the most photographed streets in Paris.

At the top of the hill (*butte*) in Montmartre is the basilica, which wasn't completed until 1919. It's named for Christ's heart, which some believe is in the crypt. You can't miss it, with its white onion domes and Byzantine and Romanesque architecture. Inside you'll find gold mosaics, but the real treat is the view of Paris from the dome or the square directly in front of the basilica. *Info*: 18th/Métro Anvers or Abbesses. place Parvis-du-Sacré-Coeur. Tel. 01/53.41.89.00. Open daily 6:45am-11pm. Observation deck and crypt 9am-6pm. Admission: Free. To the observation deck in the dome and to the crypt is 5€.

After visiting the basilica, you can head right over to the attractive **place du Tertre**. It's overrun with tourists (like you) and artists trying to paint your portrait. There's a circus-like atmosphere here, and plenty of cafés to have a snack and a drink.

After your break, you can either wander the quaint streets of Montmartre, once a small village of vineyards and windmills, or visit the **Espace Salvador-Dali**. Black walls, weird music with Dali's voice and dim lighting all make this museum an interesting experience. Come here if you're a fan of Salvador Dali to see

300 of his lithographs and etchings and 25 sculptures. *Info*: 18ᵗʰ/ Métro Abbesses. 11 rue Poulbot. Tel. 01.42.64.40.10. Open daily 10am-6pm. Admission: €10, under 8 free. www.daliparis.com.

Time for dinner. Lots of restaurants are closed on Sunday evenings. You can choose between two that are open: **Le Grand Colbert**, a stunning restaurant (*Info*: 2nd/Métro Bourse. 2 rue Vivienne [near the Place des Victoires]. Tel. 01/42.86.87.88. Closed part of Aug. Moderate) or the fun **La Maison** just south of Notre-Dame. *Info*: 5th/Métro St-Michel. 1 rue de la Bûcherie. Tel. 01/ 43.29.73.57. Closed Mon. Moderate.

After dinner visit the **Eiffel Tower**. The lines will be short, the view memorable, and the light show on the hour is spectacular. There's no better way to end your weekend in Paris! *Info*: 7ᵗʰ/ Métro Trocadéro, École Militaire or Bir-Hakeim. Champ de Mars. Tel. 01/44.11.23.23. Open daily. Elevator: Jan-Jun 15 and Sep-Dec 9:30am-11:45pm. Final ascension 11pm (10:30pm for top floor), Jun 16-Aug 9am-12:45pm. Final ascension midnight (11pm for top floor). Stairs (first and second floors): Jan-Jun 15 and Sep-Dec 9:30am-6:30pm (final admittance 6pm), Jun 16-Aug 9am-12:30am (final admittance midnight). Admission: To the first landing €4.20, second landing €7.70 and third landing €11. Stairs to the second floor €3.80, €3 under 25. www.toureiffel.fr.

WEEKEND IN PARIS / #3

Friday Evening
Head to the Bastille métro stop. The 11ᵗʰ arrondissement, centered on the place de la Bastille, is primarily a residential area that has become increasingly hip lately, especially around rue de Charonne and rue de Lappe.

When you exit the métro, you'll be at the **place de la Bastille**, but you won't

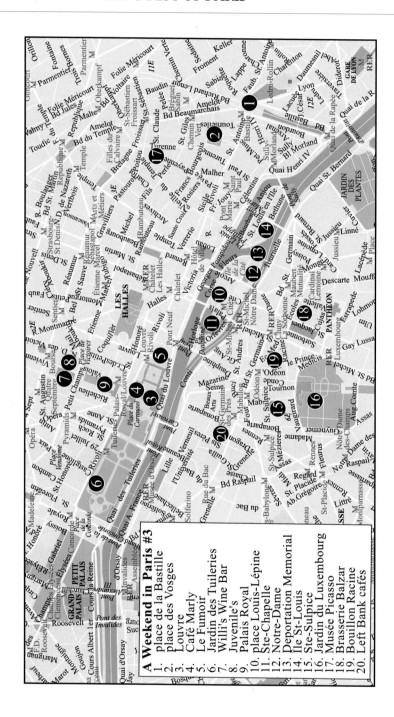

A Weekend in Paris #3
1. place de la Bastille
2. place des Vosges
3. Louvre
4. Café Marly
5. Le Fumoir
6. Jardin des Tuileries
7. Willi's Wine Bar
8. Juvenile's
9. Palais Royal
10. place Louis-Lépine
11. Ste-Chapelle
12. Notre-Dame
13. Deportation Memorial
14. Île St-Louis
15. Ste-Sulpice
16. Jardin du Luxembourg
17. Musée Picasso
18. Brasserie Balzar
19. Bouillon Racine
20. Left Bank cafés

Don't Miss ...

- dining at a bistro in the Bastille neighborhood
- exploring the Denon Wing of the Louvre
- two fabulous churches on the Île de la Cité: Notre-Dame and Ste-Chapelle
- relaxing in the Luxembourg Gardens

find it here. The notorious Bastille prison was torn down over 200 years ago when mobs stormed the Bastille as part of the French Revolution. Today, it's a roundabout traffic circle where cars speed around the 170-foot **Colonne de Jullet** (July Column). You come here for the wonderful cafés. You'll also find the **Opéra Bastille** (Bastille Opera House) on the south side of the place. Opened in 1989, this modern glass building hosts opera and symphony performances.

You have two choices for dinner (both near each other):

Bistrot Paul-Bert, a truly neighborhood bistro experience from its traditional décor to its menu written on a blackboard. (*Info*: 11th/Métro Faidherbe-Chaligny. 18 rue Paul-Bert. Tel. 01/ 43.72.24.01. Closed Sun & Mon. Moderate) or **Chez Paul**, a favorite bistro in Paris. *Info*: 11th/Métro Bastille or Ledru-Rollin. 13 rue de Charonne. Tel. 01/47.00.34.57. Moderate.

After dinner, you can do some serious people-watching back at one of the cafés on the place de la Bastille. For an even more intimate experience, you can head to the nearby **place des Vosges** (enter from rue de Birague off of rue St-Antoine). It's simply the most beautiful square in Paris, in France, and probably in all of Europe.

Saturday

We're going to visit the **Musée National du Louvre** (the "Louvre"), the world's greatest art museum. Start your day by taking the métro to the Palais-Royal stop. There are many cafés that line the rue de Rivoli near the Louvre. Try to start your day as early as possible, as the lines to enter the Louvre are shorter the earlier you arrive.

Note: It's quicker if you enter through the **Carrousel du Louvre mall** at 99 rue de Rivoli rather than through the glass pyramid.

The buildings that house the Louvre were constructed in the 13th century as a fortress. Today, the inner courtyard is the site of the controversial (but I think fantastic) glass pyramid, designed by the famous architect I.M. Pei, that serves as the main entrance to the museum.

The Louvre is the largest art museum in the world, the largest building in Paris, and it's in the largest palace in Europe.

You can get a free *Louvre Handbook* in English at the information desk under the glass pyramid. From this area, you have the choice of visiting three wings: Denon, Sully or Richelieu.

You can spend a whole weekend in the Louvre and still not see all of the art here. Your time is limited, so I've listed some highlights. Remember that even if you don't get to see the *Mona Lisa*, you'll still see incredible art. So decide how much time you want to spend here and what you don't get to see, you'll just have to come back to Paris and the Louvre again (and again)!

I suggest that you just tour the **Denon Wing** this weekend. Rooms are numbered and there are signs pointing the way to works like the *Vénus de Milo* and *Mona Lisa*. The first floor of the Denon Wing has the following incredible highlights:

- *Winged Victory of Samothrace*, a fabulous Greek statue dating back to between 220 and 190 B.C. discovered in Greece. The sculptor used marble to simulate transparent fabric over skin. (top of the Daru staircase)

- *Vénus de Milo*, the goddess of love. It dates back to 100 B.C. (room 74)
- *Mona Lisa*, painted by Leonardo da Vinci in the early 1500s (room 6)
- Directly across from the *Mona Lisa* is Veronese's *Wedding of Cana*, the Louvre's largest painting (1562)
- Huge paintings line dark red walls in room 75, including *The Coronation of Napoléon I* (1804)
- *The 28th of July 1830: Liberty Leading the People* by Delacroix (1863) (room 77)
- The Long Hall with Da Vinci's *The Virgin of the Rocks* and *John the Baptist*.

For a more detailed list of what's at the Louvre, see "A Day in the Louvre" in this book.

Info: 1st/Métro Palais-Royal. 34-36 quai du Louvre. Tel. 01/40.20.53.17 (recorded message). Open Mon, Thu, Sat-Sun 9am-6pm; Wed and Fri 9am-9:45pm. Closed Tue. Closed Jan 1, May1, Aug 15 and Dec 25. Admission: €8.50 (€6 after 6pm on Wed and Fri). Under 18 free and free the first Sunday of the month and July 14. Under 26 free after 6pm on Fri. €8.50 for exhibitions in Napoléon Hall. Combined permanent collection and temporary exhibits €13. www.louvre.fr.

When you've had enough art, you'll need a break. There are several decent cafés in the Louvre, or you could try one of these nearby places:

The **Café Marly** overlooks the pyramid at the Louvre. *Info*: 1st/Métro Musée du Louvre/Palais-Royal. 93 rue de Rivoli. Tel. 01/49.26.06.60. Open daily 8am to 2am. **Le Fumoir**, a bar and restaurant, is located near the Louvre. It's known for its Sunday brunch,

Paris Museum Pass

Don't want to wait in lines to see great art? Buy a **Paris Museum Pass** and have access to over 60 museums and monuments, including the Louvre and Musée d'Orsay. The cost is €30 for two consecutive days, €45 for four days and €60 for six days. They're available at participating museums and tourist-information centers.

salads, happy hour and *gâteau au chocolat* (chocolate cake). There's a small library in the back where you can have a glass of wine and read (you can also exchange your own books for the ones in their library). Inexpensive-Moderate. *Info*: 1ˢᵗ/Métro Louvre-Rivoli. 6 rue de l'Amiral-de Coligny. Tel. 01/42.92.00.24. Open daily 11am-2am. Closed part of Aug.

Afterwards, you can wander through the **Jardin des Tuileries**: The garden takes its name from the word *tuil* or tile (roof-tile factories once were here). You'll enjoy bubbling fountains, statues, flowers and trees between the Louvre and place de la Concorde. Sit down and relax in this beautiful garden in the middle of Paris. From here, you can also get a glimpse of the **Eiffel Tower**.

> **ALTERNATIVE PLAN**
> If you just don't want to fight the crowds at the Louvre, take the **Left Bank Walk** in the *Walks* chapter of this book. Highlights include: Musée Maillol, St-Germain-des-Prés, and the Jardin du Luxembourg.

Parisians love wine bars and so should you. Visit one of these two great wine bars for dinner: **Willi's Wine Bar**, where the British owners serve Parisian specialties (*Info*: 1st/Métro Bourse. 13 rue des Petits-Champs. Tel. 01/42.61.05.09. Closed Sun. Moderate) or **Juvenile's**, an unpretentious wine bar serving light meals. *Info*: 1st/Métro Bourse. 47 rue de Richelieu. Tel. 01/42.97.46.49. Closed Sun. Inexpensive- Moderate. Both have great wine lists.

After dinner, why don't you head to the nearby gardens of the **Palais Royal**? Built in 1632, it now houses ministries of the French government (so you won't be able to look inside). The buildings around the garden, built in the 1700s, are home to everything from stamp shops to art galleries. If you're interested in sculpture, check out the 280 controversial (meaning some did not like them) prison-

striped columns by Daniel Buren that were placed in the main courtyard. Very 80s! There are plenty of comfortable cafés here to have a nightcap. *Info*: 1ˢᵗ/Métro Palais-Royal. place Palais Royal (across the rue de Rivoli from the Louvre).

Sunday

Begin your day by taking the métro to the Cité stop. On the north side of the Île de la Cité you'll find the lovely **Marché aux Fleurs** (flower market) at **place Louis-Lépine**. On Sundays, the market becomes the **Marché aux Oiseaux** (bird market) where all types of birds, supplies and cages are sold.

You'll be on an island in the middle of the Seine River. Here, you'll be able to visit two great churches.

On a sunny day, you'll be dazzled by nearly 6,600 square feet of stained glass at **Ste-Chapelle**, a Gothic masterpiece. Fifteen windows depict biblical scenes from the Garden of Eden to the Apocalypse (the large rose window). Built in 1246, it took less than two years to build, an amazing feat when one realizes that Notre-Dame took over two centuries to complete. *Info*: 1ˢᵗ/Métro Cité. 4 boulevard du Palais. Tel. 01/53.40.60.80. Open daily Mar-Oct 9:30am-6pm, Nov-Feb 9am-5pm. Closed Jan 1, May 1 and Dec 25. Admission: €7 adults, €4 ages 18-25, under 18 free.

On the same island in the middle of the Seine River is our second sight.

The **Cathédrale Notre-Dame** is one of the greatest achievements of Gothic architecture. It's so huge that it can accommodate over 6,000 visitors. The interior is dominated by three beautiful (and immense) rose windows, and has a 7,800-pipe organ. Inside along the walls are individual chapels dedicated to saints. The most famous chapel is that of Joan of Arc in the right transept. The sacristy houses relics, manuscripts and religious garments.

You may want to climb the 387 steps of the north tower for a grand view of Paris. You'll also have a great view of the cathedral's famous gargoyles. *Info:* 4th/Métro Cité. 6 place du Parvis Notre-Dame. Tel. 01/42.34.56.10. Open daily 8am-6:45pm. Tower open daily Apr-June and Sep 9:30am-7:30pm, Jul and Aug 9am-7:30pm, Oct-Mar 10am-5:30pm. Admission: Free to the cathedral. Towers: €6, under 18 free. Treasury: €6.

After visiting these two churches, make sure you head to an overlooked sight directly behind the cathedral. Cross the street (quai Archevêché) and head through the gate.

It will take you only a short time to walk through the **Mémorial des Martyrs Français de la Déportation de 1945** (Deportation Memorial). This free memorial was built in honor of the more than 30,000 citizens who were placed on boats at this spot for deportation to concentration camps. You descend steps and become surrounded by walls. Don't miss this memorial. It's both moving and disturbing.

As you leave the memorial, exit out the gate, turn right on quai Archevêché. Head to the pedestrian bridge.

You are now on the bridge **Pont St-Louis**. Continue across this bridge to the **Île St-Louis**, a residential island within the city, often swamped with tourists during high season. The vast majority of the buildings on this island date back to the 1600s, making for a beautiful place to stroll, especially the small side streets. There are interesting shops and several good restaurants.

After you cross the bridge you'll be on the narrow **rue St-Louis-en-l'Île**, one of the most beautiful streets in all of Paris. The highlight of this street is at number 31. Tourists and Parisians alike line up at the carry-out window of **Berthillon** for the best-known ice cream in Paris. Over thirty flavors, from *chocolat blanc* (white chocolate) to *pain d'épice* (gingerbread). It's open on Sundays, except in August.

After visiting the islands, take the métro to the St-Sulpice stop.

The **Eglise St-Sulpice** is located on an attractive square with a lovely fountain (the **Fontaine-des-Quatre Points**). This church has one of the largest pipe organs in the world, with over 6,700 pipes. You'll notice that one of the two bell towers was never completed. Inside are frescoes by Delacroix in the Chapel of the Angels (Chapelle des Anges), a statue of the Virgin and Child by Pigalle, and Servandoni's Chapel of the Madonna (Chapelle de la Madone). Set into the floor of the aisle of the north-south transept is a bronze line. On the two equinoxes and the winter solstice, the sun reflects onto a globe and obelisk and from there to a crucifix. The obelisk reads: "Two scientists with God's help."

You may find fans of the wildly popular novel and movie *The Da Vinci Code* looking around the church, where it was the scene of a brutal killing. *Info*: 6th/Métro St-Sulpice. place St-Sulpice (between the boulevard St-Germain-des-Prés and the Luxembourg Gardens). Open daily. Admission: Free.

There are plenty of cafés on and around the square. Now take a short walk to the heart of the Left Bank.

The **Jardin du Luxembourg** (Luxembourg Gardens) are famous, formal French gardens filled with locals and tourists. Lots of 15th children around the pond playing with wooden sailboats. There's a replica of the Statue of Liberty in the western part of the gardens. The Statue of Liberty in New York was a gift from the French. (By the way, there's also a replica of the Statue of Liberty along the Seine River in the

15th Arrondissement at the bridge Pont de Grenelle just west of the Eiffel Tower). Also here is the **Palais du Luxembourg** (Luxembourg Palace), the home of the French Senate. Tours of the palace are by reservation only. The **Musée du Luxembourg** at 19 rue Vaugirard occupies a wing of the Palais du Luxembourg and features temporary exhibitions of some of the big names in the history of art. *Info for museum*: Tel. 01/42.34.25.95. Admission: Depends on the exhibit. *Info for gardens*: 6th/Métro Cluny-La Sorbonne. A few blocks south of boulevard St-Germain-des-Prés (off of the boulevard St Michel). Admission: Free.

Have a snack or a glass of wine at one of the cafés in the garden and relax on your Sunday in Paris.

For dinner, try one of these Left Bank institutions:

Brasserie Balzar: This *brasserie* opened in 1898 and serves traditional French cuisine. *Info*: 5th/Métro Cluny-La Sorbonne. 49 rue des Écoles. Tel. 01/43.54.13.67. Moderate.

Bouillon Racine: Popular *brasserie* serving Belgian cuisine in a historic building. *Info*: 6th/Métro Cluny-La Sorbonne or Odéon. 3 rue Racine. Tel. 01/44.32.15.60. Moderate.

ALTERNATIVE PLAN
If you had enough of visiting churches and don't want to visit a park, head to the Musée Picasso. It has the largest Picasso collection in the world (not to mention works by Renoir, Cézanne, Degas and Matisse). *Info*: 3rd/Métro St-Sébastien or St-Paul. 5 rue de Thorigny. Tel. 01/42.71.25.21. Open Apr-Sep 9:30am-6pm, Oct-Mar 9:30am-5:30pm. Closed Tue. Admission: €9.50, €7.50 ages 18-25, under 18 free. Free the first Sun of the month. www.musee-picasso.fr.

End your weekend in Paris at one of the famous cafés on the place St-Germain-des-Prés. If you're a tourist, you'll fit right in at one of Hemingway's favorite spots, **Café Les Deux Magots**. Another famous café and a favorite of tourists and Parisians alike (next door to Les Deux Magots) is **Café de Flore**. Have a drink and enjoy the great people-watching. *Info*: 6th/Métro Saint-Germain-des-Prés. Both cafés are open to at least 1am.

5. WONDERFUL ONE-WEEK PLANS

If you have more time to explore this fantastic city, you'll find three week-long plans:

Museums, Art and Architecture: The best museums, incredible art and remarkable monuments all await you in this plan.

Eating, Drinking, Shopping & Relaxing: This plan is light on museums and heavy on experiencing incredible French cuisine and wine, checking out the great shops of Paris, and relaxing at Parisian parks and cafés.

Offbeat & Off the Beaten Path: This plan takes you away from the city center so that you can experience some of the neighborhoods and sights that are off the beaten path and some sights that are just, well, offbeat!

Another option is to just pick out those plans that sound interesting and make up the perfect itinerary for you.

MUSEUMS, ART & ARCHITECTURE

Experience the best museums, incredible art and remarkable monuments in this week-long plan.

Don't Miss ...

- the fabulous **Eiffel Tower**
- **Napoléon's Tomb** at the Hôtel des Invalides
- the new **Musée du Quai Branly**

Day 1 – Exploring the Sights Around the Eiffel Tower
We'll spend the day in the area around the Eiffel Tower, home to some of the city's grandest sights, including Les Invalides and the new Musée du Quai Branly.

Take the métro to the École Militaire stop. When you exit the métro, you'll see the **École Militaire.** The Royal Military Academy was built in the mid-1700s to educate the sons of military officers. With its dome and Corinthian pillars, the building is a grand example of the French Classical style. Its most famous alumnus is Napoléon. *Info*: 7th/Métro École Militaire. Avenue La Motte-Picquet, Open to the public by special appointment.

The **Champ-de-Mars** are the long formal gardens (the "Field of Mars") that connect the **Tour Eiffel** and the **École Militaire**.

Constructed for the 1889 Universal Exhibition, the **Tour Eiffel** (Eiffel Tower) was built by the same man who designed the framework for the Statue of Liberty. It was called, among other things, an "iron monster" when it was erected. Gustave-Alexandre Eiffel never meant for his 7,000-ton tower to be permanent and

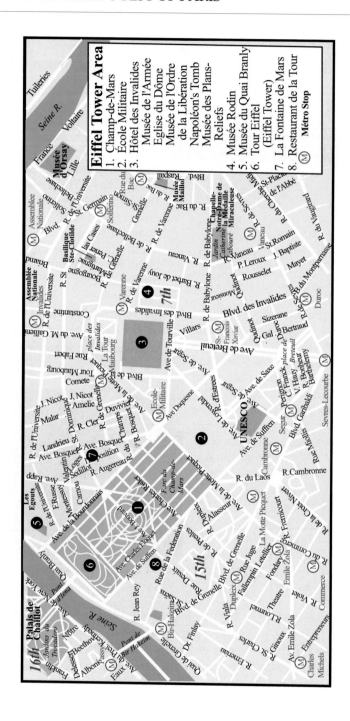

Eiffel Tower Area

1. Champ-de-Mars
2. École Militaire
3. Hôtel des Invalides
   Musée de l'Armée
   Eglise du Dôme
   Musée de l'Ordre
   de la Libération
   Napoléon's Tomb
   Musée des Plans-
   Reliefs
4. Musée Rodin
5. Musée du Quai Branly
6. Tour Eiffel
   (Eiffel Tower)
7. La Fontaine de Mars
8. Restaurant de la Tour
   Ⓜ **Métro Stop**

it almost was torn down in 1909. French radio, however, needing a broadcast tower, saved it from destruction.

Today, it's without a doubt the most recognizable structure in the world. Well over 200 million people have visited this monument. You can either take the elevator to one of three landings or climb the 1,652 stairs. You cannot visit Paris without a trip to this wonderful structure. *Info*: 7th/Métro Trocadéro, École Militaire or Bir-Hakeim. Champ-de-Mars. Tel. 01/44.11.23.23. Open daily. Elevator: Jan-Jun 15 and Sep-Dec 9:30am-11:45pm. Final ascension 11pm (10:30pm for top floor), Jun 16-Aug 9am-12:45pm. Final ascension midnight (11pm for top floor). Stairs (first and second floors): Jan-Jun 15 and Sep-Dec 9:30am-6:30pm (final admittance 6pm), Jun 16-Aug 9am-12:30am (final admittance midnight). Admission: To the first landing €4.20, second landing €7.70 and third landing €11. Stairs to the second floor €3.80, €3 under 25. www.toureiffel.fr.

You can walk over to our next sight, the **Hôtel des Invalides**.

Built in 1670 for disabled soldiers, Les Invalides with its golden dome dominates the area around it. The world's greatest military museum, **Musée de l'Armée** (Army Museum), is here (everything from battles of the 1700s through World War II), as is the second

tallest monument in Paris, the **Eglise du Dôme** (Dome Church). The main attraction here is **Napoléon's Tomb**, an enormous red stone sarcophagus. For such a tiny man, everything here is huge.

Also found here are scale models of French towns and monuments at the **Musée des Plans-Reliefs**. Napoléon is best-known for his military feats and the numerous legacies he contributed to France, including the legal code and banking system. Paris owes much of its beauty to the emperor who was responsible for many of the gorgeous monuments still standing in this city. Of course, he had them all built in his honor. *Info*: 7th/Métro Invalides or La Tour-Maubourg. 129 rue de Grenelle. Tel. 01/44.42.38.77. Open daily Oct-Mar 10am-5pm, Apr-Sep 10am-6pm. Closed first Mon of each month and Jan 1, May 1, Nov 1, Dec 25. Admission: €8, under 18 free. www.invalides.org.

Also here, and of interest to history buffs, is the **Musée de l'Ordre de la Libération**. An 18th-century mansion is the home to this museum dedicated to the Resistance and liberation of France. Included are manuscripts of General de Gaulle and exhibits on the history of the Resistance. Showcases contain uniforms, weapons, clandestine press, transmitters, and relics from the concentration camps. *Info*: 7th/Métro Invalides or La Tour-Maubourg. 51 bis boulevard de la Tour-Maubourg (enter through the Musée de l'Armée). Tel. 01/47.05.04.10. Open Apr-Sep Mon-Sat 10am-6pm, Sun 10am-6:30pm; Oct-Mar Mon-Sat 10am-5pm, Sun 10am-5:30pm Closed on the first Mon of each month, Jan 1, May 1, Jun 17, Nov 1, Nov 11 and Dec 25. Admission: €8, under 18 free (includes admission to the Army Museum, Museum of Relief Maps and Napoléon's Tomb).

There are lots of sights of interest in this area. If you have time, you should visit the new kid on the block: The **Musée du Quai Branly**. At its fabulous site along the Seine near the Eiffel Tower, this new museum is dedicated to the arts and civilizations of Africa, Asia, Oceania and the Americas. One of the walls of the museum, along Quai Branly, is completely covered with plants cascading down the walls. You have to see it. Even if you don't tour the museum, you should definitely visit the free garden. The garden café here is a good place to take a break. *Info*: 15th/Métro École Militaire or Bir-Hakeim. 37 bis Quai Branly. Tel. 0156.61.70.00. Open Tue-Sun 10am-6:30pm. Admission: €8.50. www.quaibranly.fr.

Across the river from the Eiffel Tower, the **Musée National des Arts Asiatiques – Guimet** houses a world-famous collection of Asian art. *Info*: 16th/Métro Iéna. 6 place d'Iéna. Tel. 01/56.52.53.00. Open 10am-6pm. Closed Tue. Admission: €6, under 18 free. www.musee-guimet.fr. See Major Sights West Map.

For dinner choose either **La Fontaine de Mars** (*Info*: 7th/Métro École Militaire. 129 rue St-Dominique. Tel. 01/47.05.46.44. Moderate) or **Restaurant de la Tour** (*Info*: 15th/Métro Dupleix. 6 rue Desaix. Tel. 01/43.06.04.24. Closed Sun and Mon. Moderate). Both are wonderful French dining experiences.

If you didn't take the trip up the **Eiffel Tower** during the day, you can visit it after dinner (each restaurant is near it). The lines will be short, the view memorable, and the light show on the hour is spectacular. There's no better way to end your day!

Day 2 – Famous Churches of Paris
After today's plan, you're going to be very holy! We'll see several famous churches.

Take the métro to the Cité stop. Head over to the **place du Parvis Notre-Dame** (recently renamed Parvis Notre-Dame/place Jean-Paul-II). The square in front of Notre-Dame is the center of all of France. A copper plaque on the ground outside the cathedral is **Point Zéro** from which all distances in France are measured. Tradition holds that you'll be granted a wish if you stand on this point, close your eyes and turn three times. You'll also find the entry to the **Crypte Archéologique** here. In 1965, during construction of an underground parking garage, workers discovered ruins of Roman Paris. Today, you'll find a museum instead of a parking garage. *Info*: Admission: €3.50 to the crypt, under 14 free. Crypt open 10am-6pm. Closed Mon.

To your left as you face the cathedral is the lovely exterior

Don't Miss ...

- **Notre-Dame**, one of the greatest achievements of Gothic architecture
- the dazzling stained glass at **Ste-Chapelle**
- the Left Bank's **Eglise St-Sulpice**

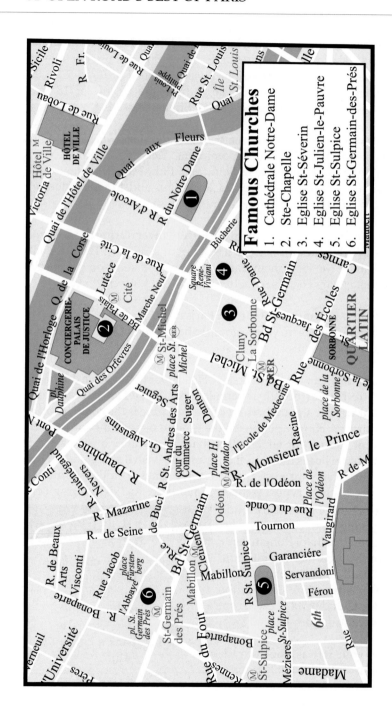

Famous Churches
1. Cathédrale Notre-Dame
2. Ste-Chapelle
3. Eglise St-Séverin
4. Eglise St-Julien-le-Pauvre
5. Eglise St-Sulpice
6. Eglise St-Germain-des-Prés

of the **Hôtel Dieu**, central Paris's main hospital. Pop into the main entrance and go straight ahead through the glass doors to view a beautiful French garden.

Before construction of the **Cathédrale Notre-Dame** began in 1163, the site was the home of a Roman temple to Jupiter, a Christian basilica, and a Romanesque church. Notre-Dame is one of the greatest achievements of Gothic architecture. Construction took nearly 200 years, and it has had a tumultuous history. Many treasures of the cathedral were destroyed at the end of the 18th century during the French Revolution. At one point, it was even used as a food warehouse.

No Halter Tops!

To gain entry to Notre-Dame and other churches in Paris, you'll need to **dress appropriately**. No halter tops, tank tops ... you get the picture, or the guards will deny you entry.

On your right when you're facing the church is the statue of Charlemagne ("Charles the Great"). On the left doorway is St. Denis holding his head. He was the first martyr of France, decapitated by a jealous king for preaching Christianity. Legend has it that he picked up his head and walked to the village of St. Denis (head in hand) where he is now buried. In the center is Christ sitting on the Throne of Judgment with those damned to hell on the right in chains and those destined for heaven on the left. The twin towers are 226 feet high. You can climb the 387 steps of the north tower for a grand view of Paris. The famous gargoyles are found between the towers. The 295-foot-tall spire was added in 1860. Along the spire's base are apostles and evangelists (and the architect looking up to his spire). On the sides of the church are the famous "flying buttresses" (50-foot beams that support the Gothic structure).

The cathedral is so huge that it can accommodate over 6,000 visitors. The interior is dominated by three beautiful (and immense) rose windows, and has a 7,800-pipe organ. Inside along the walls are individual chapels dedicated to saints. The most famous chapel is that of Joan of Arc in the right transept. The sacristy houses relics, manuscripts and religious garments. On Good Friday, what is said to be the Crown of Thorns and a piece of the cross on which Christ was crucified are put on public display. The Crown of Thorns is also displayed every 1st Friday of the month as well as Fridays during Lent. The reliquaries for the Crown (which has lost all of its thorns to different religious sites around the world) are on display daily in the treasury.

Events of note here include the crowning of Napoléon as emperor and the funeral of Charles de Gaulle.

Note: free organ recitals take place most Sunday afternoons. Although times tend to change, free tours in English are available Wednesdays and Thursdays at 2pm and Saturdays at 2:30pm. *Info*: 4th/Métro Cité. 6 place du Parvis Notre-Dame. Tel. 01/42.34.56.10. Open daily 8am-6:45pm. Tower open daily Apr-June and Sep 9:30am-7:30pm, Jul and Aug 9am-7:30pm, Oct-Mar 10am-5:30pm. Admission: Free to the cathedral. Towers: €6, under 18 free. Treasury: €6.

Also on the island is our second church:

At **Ste-Chapelle**, you'll be dazzled by nearly 6,600 square feet of stained glass at this Gothic masterpiece. The stained-glass windows owe their vibrant colors to the use of precious minerals and metals (gold for the red, cobalt for the blue). Fifteen windows depict biblical scenes from the Garden of Eden to the Apocalypse (the large rose window). The chapel was built in 1246 to house religious relics. It took less than two years to build, an amazing feat when one realizes that Notre-Dame took over two centuries to complete.

On many evenings, especially in the summer, concerts are held here. Reservations for concerts can be made by calling 01/42.77.65.65. *Info*: 1st/Métro Cité. 4 boulevard du Palais. Tel. 01/

53.40.60.80. Open daily Mar-Oct 9:30am-6pm, Nov-Feb 9am-5pm. Closed Jan 1, May 1 and Dec 25. Admission: €7 adults, €4 ages 18-25, under 18 free.

If you plan on visiting the churches on the island on another day, you can visit another church instead. The **Eglise St-Eustache** is a beautiful Gothic and Renaissance church dating back to 1532. Rembrandt's *Pilgrimage to Emmaus* is here. The church hosts contemporary art exhibits and occasional organ concerts featuring the ornate and immense pipe organ. *Info*: 2nd/Métro Les Halles. 2 rue du Jour. Tel. 01/42.36.31. 05. Open daily 9:30am-7pm. Admission: Free. See Marais Map.

There are several areas in Paris where many restaurants are concentrated in small pockets. One area is just south of the Seine River and Notre-Dame off of la rue St-Jacques in the area around la rue St-Séverin and la rue de la Huchette. Head to this area for French, Italian, Greek and other restaurants jammed into small streets. (5th/Métro St-Michel).

Still not holy enough? Two small churches in this area are near the **Square René-Viviani**, an attractive square offering one of the best views of Notre-Dame across the river:

Eglise St-Séverin was built in the early 1200s. This flamboyant Gothic church is topped by a roof featuring gargoyles, monsters and birds of prey. (The interior, with its beautiful pillars and stained glass depicting the seven sacraments, isn't bad, either.) *Info*: 5th/Métro St-Michel. rue des Prêtres-St-Séverin. Open daily. Admission: Free.

Eglise St-Julien-le-Pauvre is named after St. Julien. He was called "Le Pauvre" (the poor) because he gave all his money away. This small church is also the oldest in Paris, dating back to 1170. It's now a Greek Orthodox church. *Info*: 5th/Métro St-Michel. rue St-Julien-le-Pauvre. Open daily. Admission: Free.

After lunch, jump on the métro to the St-Sulpice stop.

The **Eglise St-Sulpice**, located on an attractive square with a lovely fountain (the **Fontaine-des-Quatre Points**), has one of the largest pipe organs in the world with over 6,700 pipes. You'll notice that one of the two bell towers was never completed. Inside are frescoes by Delacroix in the Chapel of the Angels (Chapelle des Anges), a statue of the Virgin and child by Pigalle, and Servandoni's Chapel of the Madonna (Chapelle de la Madone). Set into the floor of the aisle of the north-south transept is a bronze line. On the two equinoxes and the winter solstice, the sun reflects onto a globe and obelisk and from there to a crucifix. The obelisk reads: "Two scientists with God's help."

You may find fans of the wildly popular book *The Da Vinci Code* looking around the church. It was the scene of a brutal killing in the book. *Info*: 6th/Métro St-Sulpice. place St-Sulpice (between the boulevard St-Germain-des-Prés and the Luxembourg Gardens). Open daily. Admission: Free.

If you still haven't had enough of churches, the **Eglise St-Germain-des-Prés**, located in

ALTERNATIVE PLAN
If you like history, especially history of the royals, you may want to take an excursion to the **Basilique de St-Denis**. Saint Denis, the first bishop of Paris, was the patron saint of the monarchs. You come here to see the royal tombs. Henri II and Catherine de Médici, Louis XII and Anne de Bretagne, and Louis XVI and Marie-Antoinette are all buried here. The heart of Louis XVII, the son of Louis XVI and Marie-Antoinette, was recently placed in the royal crypt. (Who keeps these things?) *Info*: Métro Basilique St-Denis (near the end of line 13). 1 rue de la Légion d'Honneur. Tel. 01/48.09.83.54. Open daily Apr-Sep 10am-6:15pm, Oct-Mar 10am-5:15pm. Admission: €7 (to the tombs and choir).

the fashionable Left Bank neighborhood that shares its name, dates back to the 6th century. A Gothic choir, 19th-century spire and Romanesque paintings all attest to its long history. It's a frequent and beautiful site for classical concerts. *Info*: 6th/Métro St-Germain. place St-Germain-des-Prés. Open daily. Admission: Free.

For dinner, we're going to dine at a unique Left Bank restaurant near the Panthéon: **Les Papilles**. This store/restaurant sells gourmet foods and wine, and offers creative takes on classic French cuisine. *Info*: 5th/Métro Cluny-La Sorbonne (or RER Luxembourg). 30 rue Gay-Lussac. Tel. 01/43.25.20.79. Closed Sun. Moderate.

Day 3 – A Day of Contemporary Art

This day plan will expose you to some of the city's contemporary and cutting-edge art. Note that the three major museums in this day plan are closed on Tuesdays.

Start your day by heading to the Rambuteau métro stop.

You can't miss the building that houses the **Centre Georges Pompidou**. The building is a work of art in itself. Opened in 1977, the controversial building is "ekoskeletal" (all the plumbing, elevators, and ducts are exposed and brightly painted). The ducts are color-coded: blue for air conditioning, green for water, yellow for electricity,. and red for transportation. The ducts Parisians call this "Beaubourg" after the neighborhood in which it's located.

Before you head into the museum, stop in at **Café Beaubourg** facing the Pompidou Center.

The **Centre Georges Pompidou** is named after Georges Pompidou, president of France 1969-1974. This museum of 20th- and 21st-century art is a must-see. **Musée National d'Art Moderne** (The National Museum of Modern Art), the **Institut de Recherche**

Don't Miss ...

- modern art at the **Centre Georges Pompidou**
- **Musée Picasso** with the largest Picasso collection in the world
- **modern French cuisine**

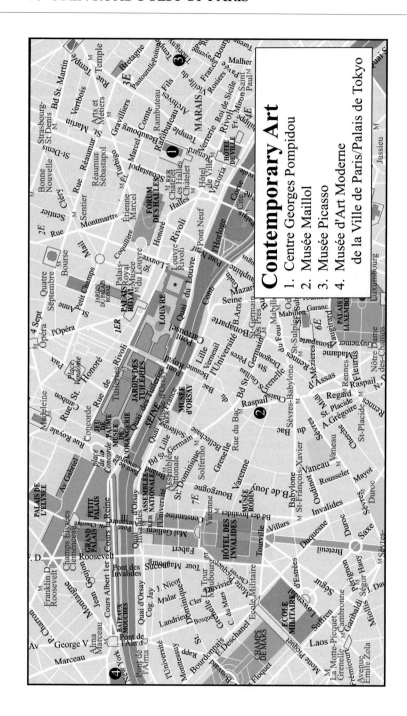

Contemporary Art

1. Centre Georges Pompidou
2. Musée Maillol
3. Musée Picasso
4. Musée d'Art Moderne
   de la Ville de Paris/Palais de Tokyo

et de Coordination Acoustique-Musique (Institute for Research and Coordination of Acoustics/Music) and the **Bibliothèque Information Publique** (Public Library) are all here. The Modern Art museum has works by Picasso, Matisse, Kandinsky, Pollock, and many other favorite modern artists. There's a great view from the rooftop restaurant (**Georges**). The **Stravinsky Fountain** and its moving mobile sculptures and circus atmosphere are found just to the south of the museum. Check out  the red pouty lips in the fountain! *Info*: 4th/Métro Rambuteau. place Georges-Pompidou (on rue St-Martin between rue Rambuteau and rue St-Merri). Tel. 01/44.78.12.33. Open Wed-Mon 11am-10pm. Closed Tue and May 1. Admission: To the Center: €10, under 18 free. Free on the first Sun of the month. www.cnac-gp.fr.

If you don't want to visit the Pompidou Center, head to a small gem of a museum, the **Musée Maillol** (Fondation Dina Vierny-Musée Maillol). The museum's permanent collection includes works of Aristide Maillol, a contemporary of Matisse, along with rare sketches by Picasso, Cézanne, Degas and other 20th-century artists. The museum also features revolving exhibits of some of the world's best-known artists. *Info*: 7th/Métro Rue du Bac. 59-61 rue de Grenelle. Tel. 01/42.22.59.58. Open 11am-6pm. Closed Tue. Admission: €8. www.museemaillol.com.

In the afternoon, you can head to another favorite museum.

Often crowded, the **Musée Picasso** has the largest Picasso collection in the world. The collection was given to the French government in lieu of death taxes. There are 1,500 drawings, 230 paintings and over 1,600 prints (not to mention works by Renoir,

Cézanne, Degas and Matisse). There's also a large collection of African masks that Picasso collected. Although there are no "masterpieces" here, this is a fine collection from every period of Picasso's artistic life. The museum is in the beautifully restored **Hôtel Salé,** which was built in the mid-1600s. The owner was a salt-tax collector (*salé* means "salty"). *Info*: 3rd/Métro St-Sébastien or St-Paul. 5 rue de Thorigny. Tel. 01/42.71.25.21. Open Apr-Sep 9:30am-6pm, Oct-Mar 9:30am-5:30pm. Closed Tue. Admission: €9.50, €7.50 ages 18-25, under 18 free. Free the first Sun of the month. www.museepicasso.fr.

If you're interested in more contemporary art, the **Musée d'Art Moderne de la Ville de Paris** houses the city's modern-art collection (including murals by Matisse), and hosts traveling exhibits. *Info*: 16th/Métro Iéna. 11 avenue du Président Wilson. Tel. 01/53.67.40.00. Open noon-8pm Tue-Sun. Admission: €5. The **Palais de Tokyo** is a contemporary art center in a colossal Art Nouveau building. *Info*: 16th/Métro Iéna. 13 avenue du Président Wilson. Tel. 01/47.23.38.86. Open noon-midnight Tue-Sun. Admission: €6. www.palaisdetokyo.com.

For dinner, try modern French cuisine (after all, you've been looking at modern art all day) at one of these two restaurants: **La Rôtisserie d'en Face,** a modern rotisserie known for its imaginative dishes (*Info*: 6th/Métro Odéon or St-Michel. 2 rue Christine. Tel. 01/43.26.40.98. Closed Sat [lunch] and Sun. Moderate) or **7ème sud Grenelle,** a small modern restaurant serving French, Mediterranean (lots of pasta dishes), and North African cuisine. *Info*: 7th/Métro La Tour-Maubourg. 159 rue de Grenelle. Tel. 01/44.18.30.30. Moderate.

Day 4 – A Day at the Louvre, the World's Greatest Museum

Take the métro to the Palais-Royal stop and start your day at one of the many cafés that line the rue de Rivoli near the Louvre. Try to start your day as early as possible as the lines to enter the Louvre are shorter the earlier you arrive.

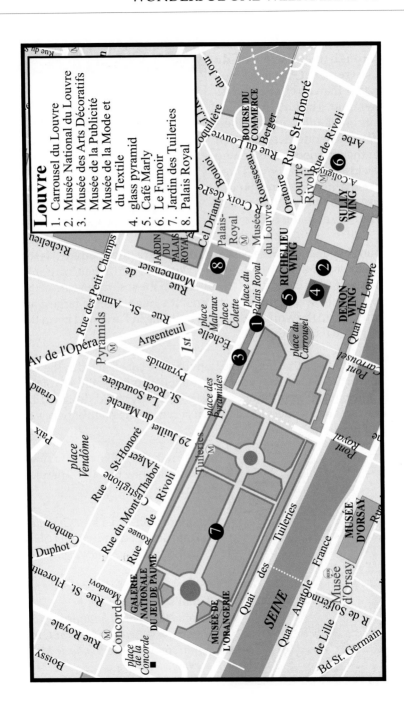

Louvre
1. Carrousel du Louvre
2. Musée National du Louvre
3. Musée des Arts Décoratifs
   Musée de la Publicité
   Musée de la Mode et
   du Textile
4. glass pyramid
5. Café Marly
6. Le Fumoir
7. Jardin des Tuileries
8. Palais Royal

Note: It's quicker if you enter through the **Carrousel du Louvre** mall at 99 rue de Rivoli rather than through the glass pyramid. The Louvre is open late on Monday and Wednesday, and is often less crowded in the afternoon. The Louvre is closed on Tuesdays. There are machines where you can use a credit card to purchase your ticket to the Louvre.

Don't Miss ...

- the **Louvre**, the largest art museum in the world and its fantastic **glass-pyramid** entrance
- relaxing in the **Jardin des Tuileries**, a beautiful garden in the middle of Paris
- a nightcap in the gardens of the **Palais Royal**

Simply put, the **Musée National du Louvre** (the "Louvre") is the greatest art museum in the world. With that said, if you have only a short stay in Paris, don't try to conquer the entire museum at the expense of seeing the rest of Paris. It's huge. It's the largest art museum in the world, the largest building in Paris, and it's in the largest palace in Europe.

The buildings that house the Louvre were constructed in the 13th century as a fortress. Today, the inner courtyard is the site of the controversial (but I think fantastic) glass pyramid designed by the famous architect I.M. Pei, that serves as the main entrance to the museum.

You'll find the following famous artworks (among the 30,000 here) at the Louvre:

- Leonardo da Vinci's *La Gioconda* (the *Mona Lisa*), *Virgin and Child with Saint Anne* and *Virgin of the Rocks*
- Michelangelo's *Esclaves* (*Slaves*)
- Titian's *Open Air Concert*
- Raphael's *La Belle Jardinière*
- Veronese's *Wedding Feast at Cana*
- not to mention the *Vénus de Milo*, *Winged Victory*...

It really doesn't matter what you see and what you don't see. Just the experience of viewing so much famous art in one place is alone worth the trip to Paris.

Here's what the Louvre has in store from top to bottom:

Second Floor:
Northern European paintings, drawings and prints; 14th- to 19th- century French paintings; and 17th- century French drawings and prints.

First Floor:
Italian-School paintings and drawings; Italian paintings (including the *Mona Lisa*); 19th- century large French paintings; Egyptian, Greek, Etruscan and Roman antiquities; and *objets d'art*.

Ground Floor:
16th- to 19th- century Italian sculptures; Islamic, Asia Minor, Egyptian, Greek, Etruscan and Roman antiquities (including *Venus de Milo*); Middle Ages and French Renaissance sculptures; and 17th- to 19th- century French and Northern European sculptures.

The Denon Wing

For a tour of the Denon Wing of the Louvre (and some of the most famous paintings in the museum), see Saturday of weekend #3 earlier in this book. Highlights include the *Mona Lisa* and *Venus de Milo*.

Below Ground Floor:
11th- to 15th- century Italian sculptures; Medieval Art; Islamic Art; Greek antiquities; and 17th- and 18th- century French sculptures.

Info: 1st/Métro Palais-Royal. 34-36 quai du Louvre. Tel. 01/40.20.53.17 (recorded message). Open Mon, Thu, Sat-Sun 9am-6pm; Wed and Fri 9am-9:45pm. Closed Tue. Closed Jan 1, May 1, Aug 15 and Dec 25. Admission: €8.50 (€6 after 6pm on Wed and Fri). Under 18 free and free the first Sunday of the month and July 14. Under 26 free after 6pm on Fri. €8.50 for exhibitions in Napoléon Hall. Combined permanent collection and temporary exhibits €13. www.louvre.fr.

Also part of the Louvre complex is the **Musée des Arts Décoratifs** (enter at #107 rue de Rivoli). Wallpaper, furniture, fabric and other decorations from the 17th century to the present are found in this special-interest museum (especially for those who are fans of Art Deco) located in the Palais du Louvre. There are Medieval, Renaissance, Art Nouveau and Art Deco rooms. It's just re-opened after a ten-year renovation. There's also a **Museum of Advertising** (Musée de la Publicité) which chronicles the history of advertising from 18th-century posters to modern-day advertising.

Also here is the **Musée de la Mode et du Textile**. This museum houses one of the largest collections of garments, accessories and textiles from the 17th century to the present. A must for those interested in fashion. *Info*: 1st/Métro Palais-Royal or Tuileries. 107 rue de Rivoli. Tel. 01/44.55.59.26. Open Tue-Fri 11am-6pm (Thu until 9pm), Sat and Sun 10am-6pm. Closed Mon. Admission: €8, €6.50 ages 18-25, under 18 free.

Hungry after all that art? The **Café Marly** overlooks the pyramid at the Louvre and is popular with visitors to the museum. The setting makes up for any complaints about the "ordinary" food. Moderate. *Info*: 1st/Métro Musée du Louvre/Palais-Royal. 93 rue de Rivoli. Tel. 01/49.26.06.60. Open daily 8am to 2am.

An alternative is **Le Fumoir**. This bar and restaurant is located near the Louvre. It's known for its Sunday brunch, salads, happy hour and *gâteau au chocolat* (chocolate cake). There's a small library in the back where you can have a glass of wine and read (you can also exchange your own books for the ones in their library). Moderate. *Info*: 1st/Métro Louvre-Rivoli 6 rue de l'Amiral-de Coligny. Tel. 01/42.92.00.24. Open daily 11am-2am. Closed part of Aug.

You need some fresh air, so head from the Louvre to the **Jardin des Tuileries**. The same man who planned the gardens of Versailles designed the Tuileries. The garden takes its name from the word *tuil* or tile (roof-tile factories once were here). You'll enjoy bubbling fountains, statues, flowers and trees between the Louvre and place de la Concorde. Sit down and relax in this beautiful garden in the middle of Paris. *Info*: 1st/Métro Tuileries or Concorde. West of the Louvre to the place de la Concorde.

You'll work up quite an appetite looking at all that art, so dine at either of these restaurants: **Le Grand Colbert**, housed in a restored historic building, serving traditional *brasserie* cuisine (*Info*: 2nd/Métro Bourse. 2 rue Vivienne [near the Place des Victoires]. Tel. 01/42.86.87.88. Closed part of Aug. Moderate) or **La Cordonnerie**, a tiny and friendly family-run restaurant near the place Vendôme serving classic French cuisine. *Info*: 1st/Métro Pyramides or Tuileries. 20 rue St-Roch. Tel. 01/42.60.17.42. Closed Sat & Sun. Moderate.

After dinner, why don't you head to the gardens of the nearby **Palais Royal**? Built in 1632, it now houses ministries of the French government (so you won't be able to look inside). You come here to take a break in the calm, beautiful garden. The buildings around the garden, built in the 1700s, are home to everything from stamp shops to art galleries. If you're interested in sculpture, check out the 280 controversial (meaning some did not like them) prison-striped columns by Daniel Buren that were placed in the main courtyard. Very 80s! There are plenty of comfortable cafés here to have a nightcap. *Info*: 1st/Métro Palais-Royal. place Palais Royal (across the rue de Rivoli from the Louvre).

Day 5 – A Day of Impressionist Art

Impressionism developed mainly in France during the late 19th and early 20th centuries. It's characterized by concentration on the general impression of an object or scene. Artists such as Renoir, Monet, Degas, Cézanne and Pissarro used small strokes and primary colors to simulate reflected light. You'll visit some of the greatest Impressionist (and Post-Impressionist) works, including the painting *Impression-Sunrise*, from which the Impressionist movement is said to have gotten its name.

Note that the **Musée d'Orsay**, **Musée de l'Orangerie** and **Musée Marmottan** are all closed on Tuesdays.

Take the métro to the Solférino stop to start your day at a magnificent museum, the **Musée d'Orsay**. Get there early to avoid the lines, and after you've entered the museum, go to the **Café des Hauteurs** on the 5th floor. The café opens at 10:30am.

This glass-roofed museum is located across the Seine from the Tuileries and the Louvre in a former train station that has been gloriously converted into 80 galleries. Many of the most famous Impressionist and Post-Impressionist works are here (on the top floor), in a building that's a work of art in itself. Some of the paintings here are:

• Monet's *Blue Water Lilies*

Don't Miss ...

• the top floor of the magnificent **Musée d'Orsay**
• Monet's *Water Lilies* at the **Musée de l'Orangerie**
• *Impression-Sunrise* at the overlooked **Musée Marmottan**

- Manet's *Olympia* and *Picnic on the Grass*
- Dega's *Absinthe*
- Renoir's *Moulin de la Galette*
- van Gogh's *Starry Night*

Impressionist Art
1. Musée d'Orsay
2. Musée de l'Orangerie

Info: 7th / Métro Solférino. 1 rue de la Légion d'Honneur. Tel. 01/40.49.48.14. Open Tue-Sun 9:30am-6pm (Thu until 9:45pm. Closed Mon, Jan 1, May 1 and Dec 25. Admission: €7.50, €5.50 ages 18-25,under 18 free. €5.50 on Sun and after 4:15pm (after 8pm on Thu). Additional €1.50 for special exhibits. www.musee-orsay.fr.

For lunch, I have two choices for you:

The **Restaurant du Musée d'Orsay** is located in the museum. There's a reasonably priced buffet lunch in an ornate dining room. Not bad for a museum restaurant. *Info*: 7th / Métro Solférino. 1 rue de la Légion d'Honneur. Tel. 01/45.49.47.03. Open for lunch. Moderate.

Not interested in dining at a museum? Try the delicious roasted chicken at **Les Deux Musées** just down the street from the Musée d'Orsay. *Info*: 7th / Métro Solférino. 5 rue Bellechasse. Tel. 01/ 45.55.13.39. Moderate.

In the afternoon, head for the **Musée de l'Orangerie**.

This former 19th-century greenhouse is situated in the beautiful Tuileries garden, and, after years of renovation, it's finally re-opened. It's home to a collection of paintings from the late 19th century and the first half of the 20th century (including 15 Cézannes, 24 Renoirs, 10 Matisses and 12 Picassos). Of particular note are *Les*

Grandes Décorations, Japanese-inspired paintings of water-lily gardens. These 22 six-foot-high canvases are stunningly displayed in two oval-shaped white rooms. *Info*: 1ˢᵗ/Métro Concorde. 1 place de la Concorde. Tel. 01/44.77.80.07. Open Wed-Mon 9am-12:30pm (groups), 12:30pm-7pm (Fri until 9pm) (individuals). Closed Tue. Admission: €7, under 18 free. Free on the first Sun of each month.

There's so much important Impressionist art in Paris that you may need to spend another day seeing it. If you have the chance, head to a jewel of a museum. It's a little out of the way, but worth the trip. The **Musée Marmottan-Claude Monet** is named after Paul Marmottan, who donated his beautiful home to house his collection of historic furnishings. In 1966, when Monet's son died in an automobile accident, the museum received over 130 works by the artist, including *Impression-Sunrise*, from which the Impressionist movement is said to have gotten its name. In addition to the well-known water lilies and paintings of his house in Giverny, you'll also see Renoir's portrait of Monet. *Info*: 16ᵗʰ/ Métro La Muette. 2 rue Louis-Boilly. Tel. 01/44.96.50.33. Open 10am-6pm. Closed Mon. Admission: €8, under 8 free. From the métro stop, walk west on Chaussée de la Muette which turns into avenue du Ranelagh. Turn right onto avenue Raphaël. The museum is on the corner of avenue Raphaël and rue Louis-Boilly. The walk from the métro stop to the museum is a half mile. www.marmottan.com. See Major Sights West Map.

Have dinner at **Aux Lyonnais**, a beautiful century-old bistro serving the cuisine of Lyon. *Info*: 2nd/Métro Bourse. 32 rue St-Marc. Tel. 01/42.96.65.04. Closed Sat (lunch), Sun & Mon. Moderate.

Day 6 – A Day of Free Museums & Sights
Two of the best **free museums** in Paris are located near each other. You can easily visit both of them in a day. Note that all the museums on this day plan are closed on Monday.

Note: Many of the museums in Paris are free (and crowded) the **first Sunday of the month**, including the Louvre and the Picasso Museum.

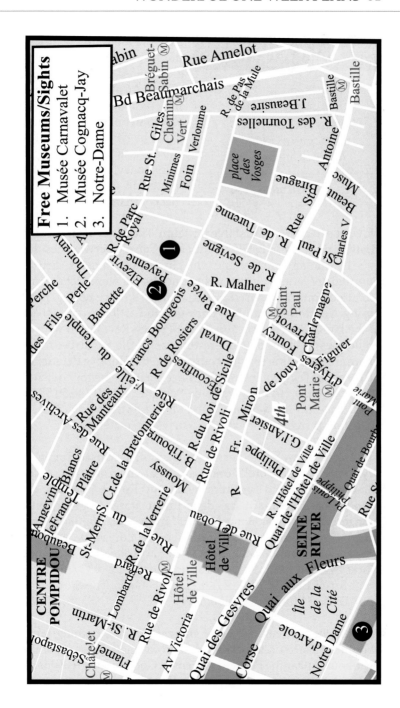

Don't Miss ...

- Parisian history at the Musée Carnavalet-Histoire de Paris
- 18th-century art at the Musée Cognacq-Jay
- Chartier, a former soup kitchen

Take the métro to the St-Paul stop. This stop is where rue de Rivoli ends and rue St-Antoine begins. All along these streets are typical cafés where you can have coffee or breakfast before you begin visiting the museums. If you're looking to save money, standing at the counter in a café (or bar) is cheaper than sitting down.

Now let's head to our first free museum: The **Musée Carnavalet-Histoire de Paris**. In the 1700s, the Hôtel Carnavalet was presided over by Madame de Sévigné who chronicled French society in hundreds of letters written to her daughter. I went kicking and screaming into this museum as it sounded so very boring. I was wrong. You'll find antiques, portraits, and artifacts dating back to the late 1700s. The section on the French Revolution with its guillotines is especially interesting, as is the royal bedroom. There are exhibits across the courtyard at the **Hôtel le Peletier de St-Fargeau**. Truly an interesting museum of the history of Paris. *Info*: 3rd/Métro St-Paul. 23 rue de Sévigné. Tel. 01/44.59.58.58. Open Tue-Sun 10am-6pm. Closed Mon. Admission: Permanent collection is free. €7 for exhibits. www.carnavalet.paris.fr.

Just a street away is another free museum. The **Musée Cognacq-Jay**, located in the **Hôtel Donon**, an elegant mansion, houses the 18th-century art and furniture owned by Ernest Cognacq, the founder of La Samaritaine department store. Cognacq once bragged that he was not a lover of art and that he had never visited the Louvre. Perhaps it was his wife, Louise Jay, who had the sense to compile such an amazing art collection, including works by Rembrandt, Fragonard and Boucher. *Info*: 3rd/Métro St-Paul. 8 rue Elzévir. Tel. 01/40.27.07.21. Open Tue-Sun 10am-6pm. Closed Mon. Admission: Free.

A good choice for lunch is **Le Hangar**. There's nothing fancy about this bistro on impasse Berthaud (a small street off of rue Beaubourg) near the Pompidou Center. Good food at reasonable prices. *Info*: 3rd/Métro Rambuteau. 12 impasse Berthaud (off of rue Beaubourg). Tel. 01/42.74.55.44. Closed Sun, Mon & Aug. No credit cards. Inexpensive-Moderate. There are plenty of other inexpensive eateries in the area around the Rambuteau métro stop.

If you're up to another free museum, head to métro Monceau.

On the edge of beautiful Parc Monceau is the **Musée Cernuschi**. Cernuschi was a banker from Milan who bequeathed his lovely home and incredible collection of Asian art to the city. A must for Asian-art aficionados. There's also a collection of Persian bronze objects. Explanatory map and notes are in English. *Info*: 8th/Métro Monceau. 7 avenue Vélasquez. Tel. 01/53.96.21.50. Open 10am-6pm. Closed Mon. Admission: Free. www.cernuschi.paris.fr. See Right Bank Picnic map.

Remember, we're trying to save money today, so for dinner you'll eat at **Chartier**, a traditional Paris soup kitchen with affordable prices. *Info*: 9th/Métro Grands Boulevards. 7 rue du Faubourg-Montmartre. Tel. 01/47.70.86.29. No reservations. Inexpensive.

End your day by heading to the **Seine River**. Walk along the river, taking in the elegantly lit **Notre-Dame** and the stunning beauty of this amazing city. And, the view is free!

Day 7 – Excursion Day: Versailles or Giverny
Today, you choose: either Versailles or Giverny.

If it's **Versailles**, take the RER train line C (from métro stops St-Michel, Gare d'Austerlitz, Invalides, Musée d'Orsay, Pont del'Alma, Javel or Champ-de-Mars) to Versailles-Rive Gauche. 40-minute trip. €5 round-trip. There's a shuttle bus (€2), but the château is a short walk.

You can also reach Versailles by SNCF trains from Gare St-Lazare and Gare-Montparnasse (10-minute walk to the château).

Bike Versailles!

Versailles is huge. A great way to get around is to **rent a bike**. Astel runs three bicycle rental stands in the park. Tel. 01/39.66.97.66.

The "Sun King" Louis XIV began construction of his splendid château in 1664. The highlights of your trip include the opulent Hall of Mirrors, the baroque **Chapelle Royale** (Royal Chapel), the queen's ornate bedroom, the marble courtyard, the royal apartments, an opera house, and the **Salon d'Apollon** (Throne Room). The famous gardens are especially beautiful in summer when the Dragon Fountain and Fountain of Neptune (along with many other fountains) gush water (Saturday and Sunday from April to September). The gardens also contain the miniature palace, the **Grand Trianon** and the beautiful mansion, the **Petit Trianon**. There is also the picturesque and charming **Hamlet** where Marie-Antoinette used to pretend that she was a peasant. Royalty!

Info: Tel. 01/30.83.78.00. Palace: Open Nov-Mar Tue-Sun 9am-5:30pm (Apr-Oct until 6:30pm). Closed Mon. Grand Trianon, Petit Trianon and Hamlet ("Domaine de Marie-Antoinette"): Open daily Nov-Mar noon-5:30pm (Apr-Oct until 6:30pm). Gardens: Open daily 7am-sunset (summer), 8am-sunset (winter). Admission to palace: €13.50, under 18 free. **Domaine de Marie-Antoinette**: €9, under 18 free. Gardens: €3 (€6 when the fountains are flowing). No credit cards. Le Passeport is the Versailles One-Day Pass (including train travel to and from Paris, audioguides, and cut-in-line privileges) April-Oct €20 Mon-Fri, €25 Sat-Sun; Nov-March €16 daily. www.chateauversailles.fr.

While you're in the park, a good choice for lunch is the informal restaurant/café **La Flotille** located on the Grand Canal. *Info*: Tel. 01/39.51.41.58. Open daily. Three-course menu is €25.

If you're not into royalty and castles, head to **Giverny**.

Trains depart Gare-St-Lazare to Vernon (the Paris-Rouen train). 50-minute trip. About €15 round-trip. 3 miles from the train station by taxi or bus.

Our destination is the **Maison et Jardin de Claude Monet** (Claude Monet House and Garden). French Impressionist painter Claude Monet lived here for 43 years and painted, among other things, the water lilies and Japanese bridges found in the beautiful gardens. Monet's green-shuttered house is now a museum. *Info*: Tel. 02/32.51.28.21. Open Apr.-Oct 9:30am-6pm. Closed Mon. Admission: €6, under 7 free.

Nearby is the **Musée d'Art Américain** (American Art Museum), dedicated to U.S.-born Impressionist artists. *Info*: Tel. 02/32.51.94.65, Open Apr.-Oct 10am-6pm. Closed Mon. Admission: €6, under 12 free. Free the first Sunday of the month.

There are cafés at both museums.

When you return to Paris, dine in splendor at **Le Grand Colbert**. You may recognize it from the movie *Something's Gotta Give* with Jack Nicholson and Diane Keaton. *Info*: 2nd/Métro Bourse. 2 rue Vivienne (near the Place des Victoires). Tel. 01/42.86.87.88. Closed part of Aug. Moderate. You can also try some excellent Italian cuisine at the elegant **Il Cortile** in the Castille hotel near the place Vendôme. *Info*: 1st/Métro Concorde or Madeleine. 33/37 rue Cambon. Tel. 01/44/58/44/58. Expensive.

EAT, DRINK. SHOP, RELAX

This next week-long plan is light on museums and heavy on experiencing **incredible French cuisine and wine,** checking out the **great shops** of Paris, and relaxing at Parisian **parks and cafés.**

Day 1 – Paris Markets & Picnics

Start your day visiting one of the many great food markets in Paris. Pick the one nearest your hotel. There's plenty of food to snack on at these markets.

Parisian markets are filled with **colorful vendors,** stinky cheese, fresh produce, poultry and hanging rabbits. Unless noted otherwise, all are open Tuesday through noon on Sunday. Some of the best-known are:

- **Rue Montorgueil** (1st/Métro Les Halles)
- **Rue Mouffetard** (5th/Métro Censier-Daubenton)
- **Rue de Buci** (6th/Métro Mabillon)
- **Rue Cler** (7th/Métro École Militaire)
- **Marché Bastille** on the **boulevard Richard Lenoir** (11th/Métro Bastille) – open Thursday and Sunday
- **Rue Daguerre** (14th/Métro Denfert-Rochereau)
- **Rue Poncelet** (17th/Métro Ternes)

Don't Miss ...

- colorful **street markets**
- tranquil **parks**

You can stock up for your picnic at the markets or try these suggestions:

On the **Left Bank**, take the métro to the Sèvres-Babylone stop.

At number 38 rue de Sèvres, you'll find **La Grande Épicerie,** the ultimate grocery store (with wine cellar and carry-out). It's located in the popular Le Bon Marché department store. Note: The grocery store is closed on Sundays. After you've stocked up, head down (south) nearby boulevard Raspail a couple blocks and turn left onto rue de Vaurgirard. Your walk is slightly less than a mile.

You'll soon run into the **Luxembourg Gardens**, where you can have your picnic. Try to find a spot near the Luxembourg Palace. Great people-watching! After your picnic, you can check out the **Musée du Luxembourg** in the Palais du Luxembourg (Luxembourg Palace). It features temporary exhibitions of some of the big names in the history of art.

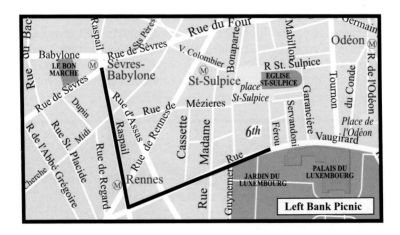

On the **Right Bank**, take the métro to the Ternes stop.

Visit the market and shops on nearby rue Poncelet. Note: The market is closed on Mondays. Don't miss Alléosse at 13 rue Poncelet, selling rare cheeses from throughout France. After

you've stocked up on picnic items, return to the Ternes métro stop and head up boulevard de Courcelles until you reach **Parc Monceau**. This tranquil park is said to be the most beautiful in the city, and it's still undiscovered by tourists. Have your picnic here surrounded by 18th- and 19th-century mansions.

If you want to visit a museum nearby after your picnic, the **Musée Nissim de Camondo** is dedicated to 18th-century *objets d'art* and furniture. Located in a mansion overlooking the beautiful Parc Monceau, it showcases objects owned by such notables as Marie-Antoinette. The kitchen of the mansion has been painstakingly restored. *Info*: 8th/Métro Monceau. 63 rue de Monceau. Tel. 01/53.89.06.50. Open 10am-5:30pm. Closed Mon-Tue. Admission: €8, under 18 free.

On the edge of beautiful Parc Monceau is the **Musée Cernuschi**. Cernuschi was a banker from Milan who bequeathed his lovely home and incredible collection of Asian art to the city. A must for Asian-art aficionados. There's also a collection of Persian bronze objects. Explanatory map and notes are in English. *Info*: 8th/Métro

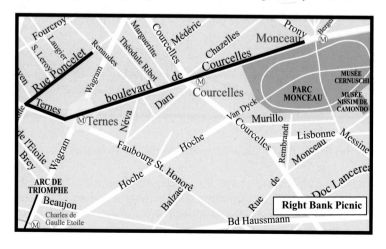

Monceau. 7 avenue Vélasquez. Tel. 01/53.96.21.50. Open 10am-6pm. Closed Mon. Admission: Free. www.cernuschi.paris.fr.

For dinner, let's keep with the outdoorsy theme. You can taste great game dishes at **Chez Maître Paul**. *Info*: 6th/Métro Odéon. 12 rue Monsieur-le-Prince. Tel. 01/43.54.74.59. Closed part of Aug. Moderate.

Day 2 – A Day at a Cooking School & Wine Tasting

Paris is the gastronomic capital of the world. If you're a lover of food and wine, this day was made for you!

This day plan may require some advance planning and reservations, so I've included websites for your convenience in arranging your day.

Start your day by taking the métro to the Champs-Élysées stop. At number 10 Champs-Élysées is **Le Pavillon Élysée**, an elegant oblong glass building built for the 1900 World's Fair. It's home to **Lenôtre**, a café, kitchen shop and cooking school all in one. A shrine to food in the heart of Paris.

Lenôtre's specialty is its desserts, and you can enjoy one with a cup of delicious coffee on the lovely stone terrace that looks onto the gardens (www.lenotre.fr).

After visiting the food shop and lingering at the café, take a cab or the métro or walk to the place de la Madeleine.

The area around the **place de la Madeleine** (8th/Métro Madeleine) is packed with fabulous specialty-food shops (the windows of the food store Fauchon are worth a trip by themselves), wine dealers, restaurants, and tea rooms. This is a perfect place for eating and purchasing culinary souvenirs. There's something for every taste-but this is an upscale area, and can be expensive. Note that most stores on the square are closed on Sunday.

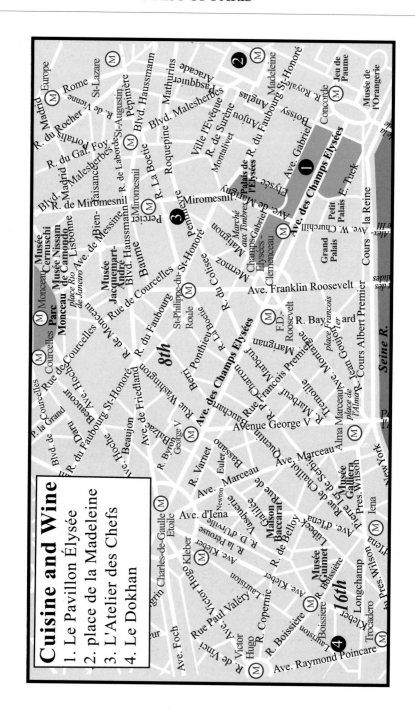

Cuisine and Wine

1. Le Pavillon Élysée
2. place de la Madeleine
3. L'Atelier des Chefs
4. Le Dokhan

The church in the middle of this square is the **Eglise de la Madeleine**. This neo-Classical church has 52 Corinthian columns and provides a great view (from the top of the monumental steps) of the place de la Concorde. Huge bronze doors depicting the Ten Commandments provide the impressive entry to the light-filled marble interior. There are three giant domes and a huge pipe organ. The painting in the chancel depicts

Don't Miss ...

- relaxing at the café at **Le Pavillon Élysée** on the Champs-Élysées
- **specialty-food shops** on the place de la Madeleine
- **cooking class** with lunch at L'Atelier des Chefs
- **wine tasting** at Ô Château
- **elegant dining**

the history of Christianity. Such grand events as the funerals of Chopin and Coco Chanel (now there's a pair!) were held here. *Info*: 8th/Métro Madeleine. place de la Madeleine. Open daily. Admission: Free.

On the east side of the church is a beautiful **flower market**. Underground are Paris's most interesting **public toilets**. Dating back to 1905, these Art Nouveau "masterpieces" have elaborate tiles, stained glass (in every stall) and beautiful carved woodwork. There's also an elaborate "throne" for shoe shining. Go even if you don't have to "go." (By the way, did you know that the female bathroom attendants are known as "Madames Pipis"?)

Now it's time to go to cooking school. Here are two choices:

L'Atelier des Chefs has half-hour cooking classes (in French, but all you have to do is follow along) with lunch. A great experience! *Info*: 8th/Métro Miromesnil. 10 rue Penthièvre. Tel. 01/53.30.05.82. Admission: €20. Reservations required. www.atelierdeschefs.com.

Paule Caillat, who speaks fluent English, operates her unique business **Promenades Gourmandes** from her apartment. Groups of six (mostly Americans) meet her at a café, visit a market to purchase ingredients for lunch, and then head to her apartment to cook a meal. It's a truly hands-on and mouth-full experience for food lovers. *Info*: 3rd/Métro Temple. 187 Rue du Temple. Tel. 01/48.04.56.84. Admission: Classes are held Tue-Fri. €215-240 for a half-day session, €310-340 for a full-day session which includes a gourmet walking tour. Gourmet walking tour without the class is €100. Reservations can be made through www.promenadesgourmandes.com.

After your cooking class, you need to taste some French wine!

"Coming to Paris and not tasting good French wines is like going to the U.S. and not trying a good burger," says Olivier Magny of **Ô Château**. This young French *sommelier* will guide you through a fun, informative and relaxing wine tasting in his Parisian loft. *Info*: 11th/Métro République. 100 rue de la Folie-Méricourt. Tel. 01/44.73.97.80. Admission: from €20 per person. www.o-chateau.com. See 10th/Canal St-Martin Map.

If you'd rather not go to a wine tasting, you can visit the **Musée du Vin**. The Wine Museum is dedicated to France's winemaking heritage. Exhibits of tools and memorabilia allow you to discover its traditions. It's located in ancient vaults and cellars dating back to the Middle Ages. Oh, and admission includes one glass of wine! *Info*: 16th/Métro Passy. 5 square Charles Dickens off of the rue des Eaux. Tel. 01/45.25.63.26. Closed Mon. Admission: 8€. www.museeduvinparis.com. See Major Sights West map.

Whatever you do in Paris, try to visit a supermarket. It's interesting to see the different foods that they have in simple markets located in department stores such as Monoprix.

Before (or after) dinner, you might want to have a glass of champagne. **Le Dokhan** (located in Trocadéro Dokhan's Hôtel) is an elegant champagne bar where you can enjoy it by the flute or by the bottle. *Info*: 16th/Métro Trocadéro. 117 rue Lauriston. Tel. 01/53.65.66.99. Open daily (evenings only).

Another choice for an *apéritif* (before-dinner drink) or *digestif* (after-dinner drink) is **Hemingway's** at the swanky Hôtel Ritz.

Dress up and expect to hand out quite a few euros for your drinks (cocktails cost €23). *Info*: 1ˢᵗ/Métro Opéra. 15 place Vendôme. Tel. 01/43.16.33.65. Open Mon-Sat 6:30pm-2am.

For dinner, head to the expensive (but not as expensive as it used to be), innovative and delicious **Senderens** (www.senderens.fr). *Info*: 8th/Métro Madeleine. 9 place de la Madeleine. Tel. 01/ 42.65.22.90. Closed weekends in July and Aug. Expensive.

Day 3 – A Day on the Left Bank
South of Île de la Cité on the Left Bank of the Seine is the **Quartier Latin** (Latin Quarter). It's a maze of small streets and squares surrounding **La Sorbonne**, the famous university. The name Latin Quarter comes from the university tradition of speaking and studying in Latin.

A great way to see the Left Bank is on the **Left Bank Walk** in the Walks Chapter of this book.

If you're not interested in the walk, start your day by taking the métro to the St-Michel stop. When you exit, you'll be at the **place St-Michel**. This much-photographed square is filled with tourists and locals. It's dominated by the ornate fountain and statue of Michael, the archangel, defeating Lucifer. It's also the site of a memorial to the liberation of France in 1944.

> ### Don't Miss ...
>
> • the **fountains** at the place St-Michel and place de la Sorbonne
> • medieval arts and crafts at the **Musée Cluny**
> • relaxing at the **Jardin du Luxembourg** (Luxembourg Gardens)
> • **cafés** on the boulevard St-Germain-des-Prés

There are plenty of cafés lining the square where you can fuel up.

Head down boulevard St-Michel until you reach boulevard St-Germain-des-Prés. On the corner, you'll find the **Musée de Cluny** (Musée National du Moyen Age/Thermes

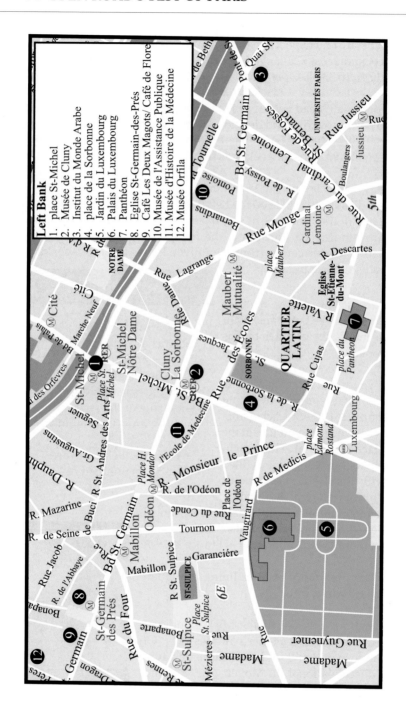

de Cluny). The building that houses this museum (the **Hôtel de Cluny**) has had many lives. It's been a Roman bathhouse in the 3rd century (you can still visit the ruins downstairs), a mansion for a religious abbot in the 15th century, a royal residence, and since 1844, a museum. It's a must if you're interested in medieval arts and crafts. Chalices, manuscripts, crosses, vestments, carvings, sculptures, and the acclaimed *Lady and the Unicorn* tapestries are all here. You enter through the cobblestoned **Cour d'Honneur** (Court of Honor) surrounded by a Gothic building with gargoyles and turrets. There's also a lovely medieval garden. *Info*: 5th/Métro Cluny-La Sorbonne. 6 place Paul-Painlevé. Tel. 01/53.73.78.16. Open Tue-Sun 9:15am-5:45pm. Closed Tue. Admission: €7, under 18 free. www.musee-moyenage.fr.

If medieval arts and crafts are not your thing, head east down boulevard St-Germain-des-Prés. At the river you'll find the **Institut du Monde Arabe** (Arab World Institute). This museum of architecture, photography, decorative arts and religion is devoted to providing insight into the Arab world. The modern building in which the museum is housed has striking traditional Arabic geometry etched  into the windows. *Info*: 5th/Métro Jussieu. 1 rue des Fossés-St-Bernard. Tel. 01/40.51.38.38. Open Tue-Sun 10am-6pm. Closed Mon. Admission: Museum: €3, under 12 free. Exhibits: €9. www.imarab.org.

Left Bank v. Right Bank

Paris is divided into two parts by the Seine River. The **Rive Gauche** (Left Bank) is to the south and the **Rive Droite** (Right Bank) is to the north. When standing on a bridge over the Seine, if the water is flowing downstream, the Right Bank is to your right.

Now head further down boulevard St-Michel until you reach the **place de la Sorbonne**. Soak up the college ambience at one of the cafés in this fountain-filled square. You're near the world-famous university **La Sorbonne**. Looking for more college atmosphere? You'll get to know your fellow diners at **Perraudin**, a bistro serving traditional Parisian cuisine at 157 rue St-Jacques.

Now you have a choice to make. If you want to relax, you can head down boulevard St-Michel to the **Jardin du Luxembourg** (Luxembourg Gardens), famous, formal French gardens filled with locals and tourists. Lots of children around the pond playing

with wooden sailboats. These gardens are referred to as the heart of the Left Bank. There seem to be birds everywhere. Ernest Hemingway, when he was destitute, is said to have come here to catch pigeons that he then strangled, cooked and ate. Also here is the **Palais du Luxembourg** (Luxembourg Palace), the home of the French Senate. Tours of the palace by reservation only. The **Musée du Luxembourg** at 19 rue Vaugirard occupies a wing of the Palais du Luxembourg and features temporary exhibitions of some of the big names in the history of art. Open daily. Tel. 01/42.34.25.95. Admission: Depends on the exhibit. *Info*: 6th/Métro Cluny-La Sorbonne. A few blocks south of boulevard St-Germain-des-Prés (off of the boulevard St Michel). Admission to the park: Free.

Not into relaxing in a park? If you're interested in French history, then you may want to head to the **Panthéon**. Originally a church, it's now the burial place for some of the greats of French history, including Voltaire, Victor Hugo, Louis Braille (who created the language for the blind) and Marie Curie (the only woman buried here). Notice the giant frescoes of the life of St. Geneviève. *Info:* 5th/Métro Cardinal Lemoine. place du Panthéon. Tel. 01/

44.32.18.00. Open daily Apr-Sep 10am-6:30pm, Oct-Mar 10am-6pm. Admission: €7, under 18 free.

And, if parks and history don't cut it, walk back up boulevard St-Michel and turn left on the famous boulevard St-Germain-des-Prés. It's lined with upscale shops. You'll soon reach the **Eglise St-Germain-des-Prés**. This church, located in the fashionable neighborhood that shares its name, dates back to the 6th century. A Gothic choir, 19th-century spire and Romanesque paintings all attest to its long history. It's a frequent and beautiful site for classical concerts. *Info*: 6th/Métro St-Germain. place St-Germain-des-Prés. Open daily. Admission: Free.

And while you're here, you have to stop in at least one of the famous **cafés** of the St-Germain-des-Prés. You've not experienced Paris unless you visit a café. Parisians still stop by their local café to meet friends, read the newspaper or just watch the world go by. You should too. It doesn't matter if you order an expensive glass of wine or just a coffee because no one will hurry you. Sitting at a café in Paris is not only a great experience, but also one of the best bargains.

On the place St-Germain-des-Prés, you'll find **Café Les Deux Magots**. If you're a tourist, you'll fit right in at one of Hemingway's favorite spots. I don't really recommend that you eat here (there's a limited menu), but have a drink and enjoy the great people-watching. Another famous café and a favorite of tourists and Parisians alike (next door to Les Deux Magots) is **Café de Flore**.

For dinner, there's something for every budget on the Left Bank.

You could try one of two relatively new players on the Left Bank gourmet scene. Get out your checkbook! You'll taste innovative dishes while dining at red-leather stools at a U-shaped bar around the kitchen at **L'Atelier de Joël Robuchon**. *Info*: 7th/Métro Rue du Bac. 5 rue de Montalembert. Tel. 01/42.22.56.56. Expensive. Reservations required. At **Gaya**, chef Pierre Gagnaire serves superb seafood at this sleek restaurant. *Info*: 7th/Métro Rue du Bac. 44 rue du Bac. Tel. 01/45.44.73.73. Closed Sun. Expensive. Reservations required.

If you're looking for something more moderately priced, try **Petit Prince**, where you'll walk through the velvet curtains and enter the intimate dining room at this friendly restaurant with an interesting crowd. *Info*: 5th/Métro Maubert-Mutualité. 12 rue de Lanneau. Tel. 01/43.54.77.26. Open daily. Moderate.

Day 4 – A Day in the Marais

The Marais is comprised of roughly the 3rd and 4th arrondissements on the Right Bank. This area, with its small streets and beautiful squares, is filled with interesting shops. It's home to both a thriving Jewish community and a large gay community. It's considered the "cœur historique," historic heart of Paris, and has retained some of the flavor of the French Renaissance.

A great way to experience the Marais is to take the **Marais Walk** in the Walks Chapter of this book.

If you'd rather not follow the walk, start your day by taking the métro to the Hôtel de Ville stop. When you get out of the métro, you'll be looking at a fantastic building. The **Hôtel de Ville** is not a hotel, it's the City Hall of Paris. Splendid, ornate and overlooking the Seine River, it's mostly closed to the public (guided tours only), but is certainly worth a look from the large fountained square in front. There are frequent free art and photography exhibits.

There are many cafés both around the Hôtel de Ville and as you head north on rue du Renard. You'll be walking in that direction to visit the **Centre Georges Pompidou** (the "Pompidou Center").

Don't Miss ...

• modern art at the **Pompidou Center**
• the largest Picasso collection in the world at the **Musée Picasso**
• he lovely **place des Vosges**

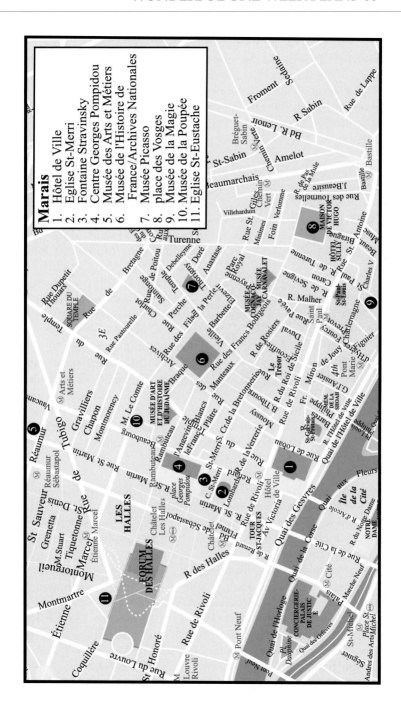

Marais

1. Hôtel de Ville
2. Eglise St-Merri
3. Fontaine Stravinsky
4. Centre Georges Pompidou
5. Musée des Arts et Métiers
6. Musée de l'Histoire de France/Archives Nationales
7. Musée Picasso
8. place des Vosges
9. Musée de la Magie
10. Musée de la Poupée
11. Eglise St-Eustache

On your way to the **Pompidou Center**, you'll pass **Eglise St-Merri** at 78 rue St-Martin. Pop inside. This church dates from the mid-16th century and has a flamboyant Gothic exterior (including lots of gargoyles). Its interior isn't bad, either. Lots of stained glass and a famous wooden organ. The composer Saint-Saëns was once an organist here. The church bell is said to be the oldest in Paris.

Between the Eglise St-Merri and the Pompidou Center is an interesting fountain.

The **Fontaine Stravinsky** (Stravinsky Fountain) and its moving mobile sculptures and circus atmosphere are found just to the

south of the museum. Check out the red pouty lips in the fountain! This is a crowded, energetic and popular area filled with shops of all kinds. If you're interested in having lunch, you can stop at the trendy **Café Beaubourg** over-looking the museum or the in-expensive **Le Hangar** on im-passe Berthaud (off of rue Beaubourg). *Info*: 3rd/Métro Rambuteau. 12 impasse Berthaud (off of rue Beaubourg). Tel. 01/42.74.55.44. Closed Sun, Mon & Aug. No credit cards. Inexpensive-Moderate.

Now, head to the Pompidou Center. This museum of 20th- and 21st-century art is a must-see. The building is a work of art in itself. Opened in 1977, the controversial building is "ekoskeletal" (all the plumbing, elevators, and ducts are exposed and brightly painted). The ducts are color-coded: blue for air conditioning, green for water, yellow for electricity, and red for transportation. Parisians call this "Beaubourg" after the neighborhood in which it's located. **Musée National d'Art Moderne** (The National Museum of Modern Art) has works by Picasso, Matisse, Kandinsky, Pollock, and many other favorite modern artists. There's a great view from the rooftop restaurant (**Georges**). *Info*: 4th/Métro Rambuteau. place Georges-Pompidou (on rue St-Martin between rue Rambuteau and rue St-Merri). Tel. 01/44.78.12.33. Open Wed-Mon 11am-10pm. Closed Tue and May 1. Admission: To the Center: €10, under 18 free. Free on the first Sun of the month. www.cnac-gp.fr.

A walk from the Pompidou Center east on rue Rambuteau, which turns into rue des Francs-Bourgeois, will give you a good feel for the Marais.

If you're more into science than contemporary art, you can continue north to visit

Best Fountains

• the ornate fountain and statue of St. Michael at the **place St-Michel**
• the fountains at the huge **place de la Concorde**
• the fun **Fontaine Stravinsky** at the Pompidou Center
• the majestic fountains at **Versailles**

the **Musée des Arts et Métiers.** It's a huge interactive museum of science and industry. It's located in the former church of St-Martin des Champs. *Info*: 3rd/Métro Arts et Métiers. 60 rue Réaumur. Tel. 01/53.01.82.00. Open Tue-Sun 10am-6pm (Thu until 9:30pm). Closed Mon. Admission: €6.50, under 18 free. www.arts-et-metiers.net.

If you're looking for a place to eat lunch near the science and industry museum, try **Au Bascou,** a modern bistro serving Basque specialties. *Info*: 3rd/Métro Arts-et-Métiers. 38 rue Réaumur. Tel. 01/42.72.69.25. Closed Sat (lunch), Sun, Mon (lunch), and Aug. Moderate.

Walk down rue des Francs-Bourgeois and you'll pass shops and the **Musée de l'Histoire de France/Musée des Archives Nationales** at number 60. This museum houses France's most famous documents, including some written by Joan of Arc, Marie-Antoinette and Napoléon. It's located in the **Hôtel de Clisson,** a palace dating back to 1371, the highlight of which is the incredibly ornate, oval-shaped **Salon Ovale.** *Info*: 3rd/Métro Hôtel de Ville. 60 rue des Francs-Bourgeois. Tel. 01/40.27.60.96. Mon and Wed-Fri 10am-12:30pm and 2pm-5:30pm, Sat-Sun 2pm-5:30pm. Closed Tue. Admission: €3, under 18 free.

You'll also pass both the free **Musée Cognacq-Jay** and **Musée Carnavalet** (both featured in "A Day of Free Museums and Sights" in this book).

But, today you're heading to the most popular museum in the Marais. The **Musée Picasso** has the largest Picasso collection in  the world. The collection was given to the French government in lieu of death taxes. There are 1,500 drawings, 230 paintings and over 1,600 prints (not to mention works by Renoir, Cézanne, Degas and Matisse). There's also a large collection of African masks that Picasso collected. Although there are no "masterpieces" here, this is a fine collection from every period of Picasso's artistic life. The museum is in the beautifully restored **Hôtel Salé,** which was built in the mid-1600s. The owner was a salt-tax collector (*salé* means "salty"). *Info*: 3rd/Métro St-Sébastien or St-Paul. 5 rue de Thorigny. Tel. 01/42.71.25.21. Open Apr-Sep 9:30am-6pm, Oct-Mar 9:30am-5:30pm. Closed Tue. Admission: €9.50, €7.50 ages 18-25, under 18 free. Free the first Sun of the month. www.musee-picasso.fr.

If you continue walking down rue des Francs-Bourgeois, you'll run into the **place des Vosges**. It's simply the most beautiful square in Paris, in France, and probably in all of Europe. It's the oldest square in Paris, a beautiful and quiet park surrounded by stone and red-brick houses. Upscale boutiques are found in the attractive arcades. The square is also known as la place Royale, as it was designed for royal festivities. Don't miss it!

At the square is the **Maison de Victor Hugo** (Victor Hugo's House). You can't seem to go anywhere in this city without seeing the name of Victor Hugo (he wrote *Les Misérables* and *The Hunchback of Notre Dame*). This 19th-century literary legend's home is now a museum. Hugo was also an artist, and you can view 350 of his drawings here. *Info*: 4th/Métro St-Paul or Bastille. 6 place des Vosges. Tel. 01/42.72.10.16. Open Tue-Sun 10am-5:30pm. Closed Mon. Admission: €6.

For dinner, you can have a true Marais experience at **Au Gamin de Paris**, a small Marais bar/restaurant serving Parisian specialties. *Info*: 4th/Métro Saint-Paul. 51 rue Vieille du Temple. Tel. 01/42.78.97.24. Moderate. If you're up for Italian food, try **L'Enoteca**, an attractive Italian wine bar/bistro. *Info*: 4th/Métro St-Paul. 25 rue Charles V (at rue St-Paul). Tel. 01/42.78.91.44. Closed part of Aug. Moderate.

After dinner, visit **Le Trésor** where cocktails are served both inside and outside at tables along a lovely, flowered street in the heart of the Marais. Great people-watching. *Info*: 4th/Métro Hôtel de Ville or Saint-Paul. 5-7 rue du Trésor (off of rue Vieille du Temple). Tel. 01/42.71.35.17.

The **Marais** is home to a thriving Jewish community. **Rue des Rosiers** is a great place to get a falafel sandwich and to view shop windows filled with Jewish artifacts. Two important Jewish sights are found in the Marais and worth a visit, and try to visit the great deli shop below as well:

Mémorial de la Shoah: Holocaust memorial featuring a wall containing the names of the 76,000 who were deported to concentration camps. *Info*: 4th/Métro St-Paul. 17 rue Geoffroy-l'Asnier. Tel. 01/42.77.44.72. Open 10am-6pm. Closed Sat. Admission: Free. Temporary exhibits €6.

Musée d'Art et d'Histoire du Judaïsme: A museum of Jewish art and history. *Info*: 3rd/Métro Rambuteau. 71 rue du Temple. Tel. 01/53.01.86.60. Open Mon-Fri 11am-6pm, Sun 10am-6pm. Closed Sat. Admission: €7, under 18 free.

Chez Marianne: Popular, charming take-away deli (you can also eat here) featuring authentic Jewish specialties. Inexpensive. *Info*: 4th/Métro St-Paul. 2 rue des Hospitalières-St-Gervais. Tel. 01/42.72.18.86.

Day 5 – Shopping (and Museums) Around the Opéra
The 9th Arrondissement is home to the opulent Opéra Garnier, a center for shopping (most major department stores are here), and a mecca for nightlife.

Start your day by taking the métro to the Opéra stop.

You can begin your day in style at the elegant **Café de la Paix** on the square (the place de l'Opéra). *Info*: 9th/Métro Opéra. 12 boulevard des Capucines (place de l'Opéra). Tel. 01/40.07.30.20.

On the square (the place de l'Opéra) is the **Opéra Garnier**. Built in 1875, this ornate opera house is now the showplace for both

opera and dance. It's often referred to as the most opulent theater in the world. Chandeliers, marble stairways, red-velvet boxes, a ceiling painted by Chagall, and a facade of marble and sculpture make this the perfect place for an elegant night out in Paris. There's also a museum celebrating opera and dance over the years. *Info*: 9th/Métro Opéra. place de l'Opéra. Tel. 01/40.01.22.63. Open daily 10am-5pm. Admission: €7.

Nearby is the **Musée de la Parfumerie-Fragonard**. Located in a lovely 1860 town house, this museum is devoted to the history of perfume from the time of the Egyptians to today. *Info*: 9th/Métro Opéra. 9 rue Scribe. Tel. 01/47.42.04.56. Open Mon-Sat 9am-6pm, Sun 9:30am-4pm from Mar 15-Oct 15, and Dec 15-Jan 15. Admission: Free.

If you're not into opera or perfume, visit **Paris-Story**. Okay, so it's really touristy. This 45-minute multimedia show is a good introduction to what

> **Don't Miss ...**
>
> • the opulent **Opéra Garnier**
> • shopping at the **department stores** on boulevard Haussmann
> • a nightcap at the lovely **Café de la Paix**

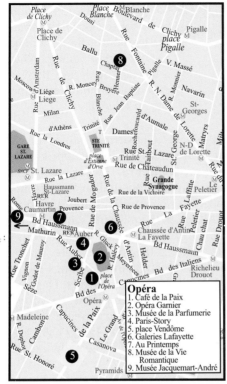

Opéra
1. Café de la Paix
2. Opéra Garnier
3. Musée de la Parfumerie
4. Paris-Story
5. place Vendôme
6. Galeries Lafayette
7. Au Printemps
8. Musée de la Vie Romantique
9. Musée Jacquemart-André

Paris has to offer and is an interesting educational experience (especially for children), as it highlights the history of the city. Headphones provide translations in 12 languages. *Info*: 9th/Métro Opéra. 11 bis rue Scribe. Tel. 01/42.66.62.06. Open daily. Shows hourly 9am-7pm. Admission: €10, €6 ages 6-18, under 6 free. www.paris-story.com.

Now it's time to shop!

Just off the place de l'Opéra is the **place Vendôme**. This elegant square is the home of a 144-foot column honoring Napoléon. You'll find world-famous jewelers here, and great shopping for those with lots of disposable income.

Boulevard Haussmann (just off the place de l'Opéra) is the home to the top two department stores in Paris. **Galeries Lafayette** at 40 blvd. Haussmann (9th/ Métro Chaussée d'Antin) opened in 1894. You'll find designer clothes, a wonderful food hall and a free view of Paris from the 7th floor. **Au Printemps** at 64 blvd. Haussmann (9th/ Métro Havre-Caumartin) opened in 1864. Here,

Beautify at Au Printemps!

Two levels of **Au Printemps** are devoted to beauty supplies and treatments.

you'll find designer clothing, household goods and furniture. The tearoom on the 6th floor has a stained-glass ceiling. Which is better? You decide. Both are closed on Sundays and open late on Thursdays.

For lunch, if you don't want to eat at a department store, you can head to the nearby **Musée Jacquemart-André**. Among the department stores and shops on boulevard Haussmann is this museum featuring art, especially from the Italian Renaissance. Jacquemart and André collected rare paintings and decorative art in this 1850s mansion. Although the museum with its paintings by Rembrandt, Bellini, Carpaccio, Van Dyck and Rubens is memorable, the opulent mansion is the real star here. Marble staircases, chandeliers and elaborately painted ceilings vie for your attention rather than the paintings on the walls. The high-ceilinged dining room, with its 18th-century tapestries, is a popular place to rest and have tea, a salad or pastry. *Info*: 8th/Métro Miromesnil. 158 boulevard Haussmann. Tel. 01/45.62.11.59. Open daily 10am-6pm. Admission: €9.50, under 7 free.www.musee-jacquemart-andre.com.

One other museum of note near here is the **Musée de la Vie Romantique**. Housed in an Italianate villa, the first floor showcases the personal effects of novelist George Sand, including her watercolors. The second floor is devoted to the collection of painter Ary Scheffer of the Romantic movement (from which the museum takes its name). The museum is lovely, especially the garden and greenhouse. *Info*: 9th/Métro Blanche. 16 rue Chaptal. Tel. 01/55.31.95.67. Open 10am-6pm. Closed Mon. Admission: Permanent collection is free.

For dinner, try either **Au Petit Riche**, a bistro that serves specialties of the Loire Valley with a Parisian twist (*Info*: 9th/Métro Le Peletier. 25 rue Le Peletier at rue Rossini. Tel. 01/47.70.68.68. Closed Sun. Moderate) or **Bistro de Deux Théâtres** for affordable dining at a neighborhood bistro. *Info*: 9th/Métro Trinité. 18 rue Blanche. Tel. 01/45.26.41.43. Moderate.

Consider heading back to the **Café de la Paix** on the square (the place de l'Opéra) for a nightcap. It overlooks the opera house which is especially lovely when lit at night.

Another choice for a *digestif* (after-dinner drink) is **Hemingway's** at the swanky Hôtel Ritz on the **place Vendôme**. Dress up and expect to hand out quite a few euros for your drinks (cocktails cost €23). *Info*: 1ˢᵗ/Métro Opéra. 15 place Vendôme. Tel. 01/43.16.33.65. Open Mon-Sat 6:30pm-2am

Day 6 – Paris with Kids
Start your day by taking the métro to the rue du Bac stop. At 46 rue du Bac you'll find **Deyrolle**, a taxidermy shop "stuffed" with

everything from snakes to baby elephants to zebras. Also on display are collections of butterflies, shells and minerals from all over the world. Kids seem to love this place. You have to go upstairs! The shop also sells planters, clothes and other household items (some  modeled on the stuffed animals). Very quirky! It's closed on Sunday. See Left Bank Walk Map.

Kids can be picky (oh, you didn't know that?) and have strong likes and dislikes, so you have several choices depending on your children's interest.

If your kids are interested in science, you might want to head to the **Musée National d'Histoire Naturelle** (National Museum of Natural History). Visit the Gallery of the Evolution of Man and exhibits on everything from entomology (the study of insects) to paleontology (the study of dinosaurs). You'll be greeted by a huge whale skeleton. (You may want to skip the skeletons of fetuses and Siamese twins.) *Info*: 5ᵗʰ/Métro Jussieu. 57 rue Cuvier. Tel. 01/40.79.30.00. Open 10am-5pm. Closed Tue. Admission: €7, €5 ages 4-16 and over 60, under 4 free. See "No Tourist Day" Map.

If you've got a future pilot or flight attendant in your family, why not head to the **Musée de l'Air et de l'Espace**? Air, space and balloon travel is explored at this new museum in the former passenger terminal at Le Bourget airport. Among the 150 aircraft here is the prototype for the Concorde. *Info*: Aéroport de Paris-Le Bourget. Métro Gare du Nord and then bus #350. Tel. 01/49.92.70.62. Open Oct-Mar Tue-Sun 10am-5pm (Apr-Sep until 6pm). Admission: €7, under 18 free. www.mae.org.

If your kids like dolls, you can visit the **Musée de la Poupée** (Doll Museum). This museum displays over 200 dolls produced in France from the 1800s to today. There's also a gift shop for all doll lovers. *Info*: 3ʳᵈ/Métro Rambuteau. Impasse Berthaud (off of 22 rue Beaubourg). Tel. 01/42.72.55.90. Open Tue-Sun 10am-6pm. Closed Mon. Admission: €6, €4 ages 3-18, under 3 free. www.museedelapoupeeparis.com. See Marais Map.

On Wednesday, Saturday and Sunday afternoons, you can visit the **Musée de la Magie** (Museum of Magic). This museum is located in rooms made to look like caves. It's filled with over 3,000 magic props (like an early sawing-a-person-in-half box, trick cards and vibrating tables). Tours are in English and French. A live magic show is included. *Info*: 4ᵗʰ/Métro St-Paul. 11 rue St-Paul. Tel. 01/42.72.13.26. Open Wed, Sat-Sun 2pm-7pm. Admission: €7. www.museedelamagie.com. See Marais Map.

Interested in going to a French amusement park? You can head to the **Jardin d'Acclimatation**. The northern 25 acres of the **Bois de Boulogne** (an enormous park of nearly 2,200 acres) is just the place for kids (except at night). On Wednesdays, Saturdays and Sundays take a ride on the yellow-and-green train to the amuse-

ment-park entrance from the Porte Maillot métro stop, which departs every 30 minutes (€5). Playgrounds, pony rides, a zoo, miniature golf course, bowling alleys, a hall of mirrors …you get the picture. La Prévention Routière is probably the most interesting

ing attraction. It's a miniature roadway where children drive small cars. Real police officers (*gendarmes*) teach kids to follow and obey stoplights and street signs. *Info*: 16th/Métro Porte Maillot. Tel. 01/40.67.90.82. Open daily Jun-Sep 10am-7pm (Oct-May until 6pm). Admission: €3, under 3 free. See Major Sights West Map.

The biggest tourist attraction in France (even greater than the Eiffel Tower) is **Disneyland Paris**. The French Disneyland isn't much different than the Disney parks in the U.S. Main Street USA, Adventureland, Frontierland, Fantasyland and Discoveryland are all here. **Village Disney** is a free entertainment area with restaurants, bars and clubs. **Walt Disney Studios** (an interactive film studio) is next to Disneyland (separate admission charge). *Info*: Take the RER line A (from many métro stops such as Nation, Châtelet-Les Halles or Charles-de-Gaulle-Étoile) to Marne-la Vallée/Chessy. 45-minute trip. Fare is €13 round-trip. Tel. 01/60.30.60.53. Open daily 10am-8pm. One-day admission to Disneyland is €42 for adults, €34 ages 3-1, under 3 free. Package deals available. www.disneylandparis.com.

For dinner, take the kids to the family-friendly **Soprano**, an Italian restaurant in the Marais. *Info*: 4th/Métro St-Paul. 5 rue Caron. Tel. 01/42.72.37.21. Inexpensive-Moderate. An alternative would be to eat at **Hippopotamus**, a chain of inexpensive restaurants with over twenty locations in Paris. Kids love it.

Day 7 – Excursion Day: Chartres or Chantilly
We'll get away from bustling Paris today and head for **Chartres**.

Trains from Gare Montparnasse to Chartres. About an hour trip. About €25 round-trip.

The gothic **Cathédrale Notre-Dame de Chartres** with its two tall spires, world-famous stained glass windows and its **Royal Portal**, three sculpted doorways, is a popular day trip from Paris. The picturesque **Vieux Quartier** (old town) is quite different from bustling Paris. *Info*: Tel. 02/37.21.75.02. Cathedral: Open daily 8:30am-6:45pm. Admission: Free. Malcolm Miller conducts excellent tours in English for €10 (Tel. 02/37.28.15.58 or millershartres@aol.com). Meet at cathedral gift shop, daily noon and 2:45pm, except Sun.

If you'd rather see a castle than a cathedral, head to **Chantilly**.

Trains from Gare du Nord to Chantilly-Gouvieux daily. 30-minute trip. You can take a cab to the *château* (€6) or the free "Senlis" bus to the Chantilly-Eglise Notre-Dame stop.

Chantilly makes for a relaxing day trip from Paris. The picturesque village is the site of the magnificent **Château de Chantilly**, which dates back to the 1600s and was restored in the 19th century. It's the home of the **Musée Condé** (Condé Museum), known for its tapestries. *Info*: Tel. 03/44.62.62.62. Open Nov-Mar 10:30-5pm (Apr-Nov until 6pm). Closed Tue. Admission: €8, under 18 free. www.chateaudechantilly.com.

Horse lovers will want to visit the **Grandes Écuries** (Great Stables) and its **Musée Vivant du Cheval** (Horse Museum). *Info*: Tel. 03/44.57.40.40 Closed Tue, Admission: €9.

When you return to Paris, have dinner at **Chardenoux**, a small, friendly restaurant serving traditional Parisian cooking. *Info*: 11th/Métro Charonne. 1 rue Jules-Vallès and 23 rue Chanzy. Tel. 01/43.71.49.52. Closed Sat (lunch), Sun & part of Aug. Moderate.

OFFBEAT & OFF THE BEATEN PATH

This plan takes you away from the city center. Experience some of the neighborhoods and sights that are off the beaten path and some sights that are just, well, offbeat!

Day 1 – Montmartre

Once a small village of vineyards and windmills, Montmartre is dominated by the massive Sacred Heart Basilica. It's also home to the sleazy place Pigalle.

An easy way to see Montmartre is to take the **Montmartre Walk** found in the *Walks* chapter of this book.

If you're not interested in taking the walk, start your day by taking the métro to the Abbesses stop.

The **place des Abbesses** is a picturesque triangular "square" and features one of the few remaining curvy Art Nouveau entrances to the Abbesses métro stop. This métro stop is the deepest in Paris, and stands on the site of a medieval abbey.

Don't Miss ...

- the **Basilique du Sacré-Coeur** (Sacred Heart Basilica) and its *incroyable* views
- the circus-like atmosphere at **place du Tertre**
- the interesting **Espace Salvador-Dali**

We'll start our day by visiting two churches. First we'll visit the **Basilique du Sacré-Coeur** (Sacred Heart Basilica).

To avoid climbing the hundreds of steps to the Basilica, follow the signs to the funicular (cable car), which will take you up to the Basilica for the price of a métro ticket.

You could also head directly up **Rue Foyatier**. With over 200 steps, this "street" is west (left) of the hill leading up to Sacré-

Coeur. It is one of the most photographed streets in Paris.

At the top of the hill (*butte*) in Montmartre is the Basilica of the Sacred Heart, which wasn't completed until 1919. It's named for

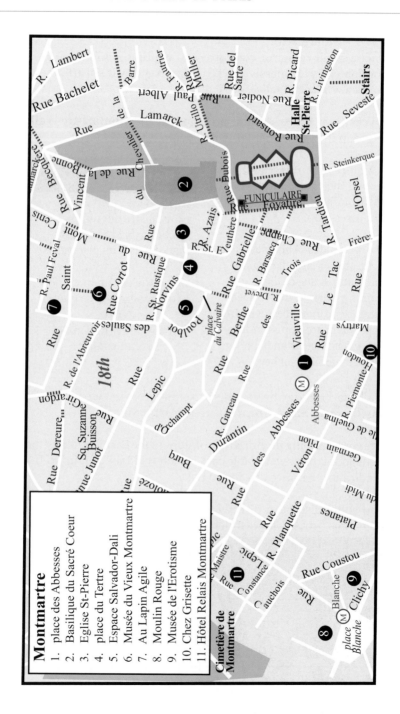

Montmartre
1. place des Abbesses
2. Basilique du Sacré Coeur
3. Eglise St-Pierre
4. place du Tertre
5. Espace Salvador-Dali
6. Musée du Vieux Montmartre
7. Au Lapin Agile
8. Moulin Rouge
9. Musée de l'Erotisme
10. Chez Grisette
11. Hôtel Relais Montmartre

Christ's heart which some believe is in the crypt. You can't miss it with its white onion domes and Byzantine and Romanesque architecture. Inside you'll find gold mosaics, but the real treat is the view of Paris from the dome or the square directly in front of the basilica. *Info*: 18th/Métro Anvers or Abbesses. place Parvis-du-Sacré-Coeur. Tel. 01/53.41.89.00. Open daily 6:45am-11pm. Observation deck and crypt 9am-6pm. Admission: Free. To the observation deck in the dome and to the crypt is 5€.

To the west side of the basilica is another church that you can just pop into: The **Eglise St-Pierre**, one of the oldest churches in Paris in the shadows of Sacré-Coeur. The Roman marble columns date back to the 1100s.

Now follow the crowds to a popular Montmartre square.

The **place du Tertre** is west of Sacré-Coeur. It's filled with tourists and artists trying to paint your portrait. You can take a break here at one of the touristy cafés and then head to a museum.

I'll give you two very different choices for museums. Black walls, weird music with Dali's voice and dim lighting all make **Espace Salvador-Dali** an interesting experience. Come here if you're a fan of Salvador Dali to see 300 of his lithographs and etchings and 25 sculptures. *Info*: 18th/Métro Abbesses. 11 rue Poulbot. Tel. 01.42.64.40.10. Open daily 10am-6pm. Admission: €10, under 8 free. www.daliparis.com.

If you're not interested in Dali's works, you can visit the nearby **Musée du Vieux Montmartre**. Renoir and van Gogh are just a few of the artists who have occupied this 17th-century house. It's now a museum with a collection of mementos of this neighborhood, including paintings, posters and photographs. *Info*: 18th/Métro Anvers. 12 rue Cortot. Tel. 01/49.25.89.37. Open Tue-Sun 10am-6pm. Closed Mon. Admission: €7, under 10 free. www.museedemontmartre.fr.

For dinner, you'll be dining at **Chez Grisette** in the heart of Montmartre. The English-speaking and very friendly owner manages to take care of all of the 24 people she can squeeze into her restaurant. *Info*: 18th/Métro Abbesses or Pigalle. 14 rue Houdon. Tel. 01/42.62.04.80. Closed Sat & Sun. No lunch. Inexpensive – Moderate.

You've seen the movie, now see the cancan. Originally a red windmill, the **Moulin Rouge** dance hall has been around since

1889. It's without a doubt the most famous cabaret in the world. Toulouse-Lautrec memorialized the Moulin Rouge in his paintings. Looking for a little bit of Vegas? You'll find it here. *Info*: 18th/Métro Blanche. 82 boulevard de Clichy. Tel. 01/53.09.82.82. Shows nightly at 9pm and 11pm. Admission: €87 (11pm show with half bottle of champagne). €140-170 (7pm dinner followed by 9pm show). www.moulinrouge.fr.

After dinner, you can walk to the **Basilique du Sacré-Coeur** (Sacred Heart Basilica) where you'll have a great view of Paris from the square in front of the basilica.

You may want to end your evening at **Au Lapin Agile**. You'll hear French folk tunes at this shuttered cottage at the picturesque intersection of rue des Saules and rue St-Vincent. It was once frequented by Picasso. You'll sit at small wooden tables and listen to *chansonniers* (singers). Truly a Parisian experience. *Info*: 18th/Métro Lamarck-Caulaincourt. Intersection of rue des Saules and rue St-Vincent. Tel. 01/46.06.85.87. Open Tue-Sun 9pm-2am. Closed Mon. Admission: €24 (includes a drink). No credit cards. Reservations can be made at www.au-lapin-agile.com.

And if you're really a late-night, adventurous type, you can head to the sleazy place Pigalle. You come here for only one thing: sex. Littered with sex shops, this area was known as "Pig Alley" during World War II. While here, you can visit yet another museum (of a different sort). The **Musée de l'Erotisme** (Museum of Erotic Art) is devoted to erotic art. 2,000 paintings, photos, carvings (can you say "dildo"?), implements ... Well, you get the picture. Not surprisingly, the museum remains open until the wee hours of the morning. There's also a "gift" shop, of course. *Info*: 18th/Métro Blanche. 72 blvd. de Clichy. Tel. 01.42.58.28.73. Open daily 10am-2am. Admission: €8. www.musee-erotisme.com.

Day 2 – The 10th Arrondissement: Canal St-Martin
Begin your day by taking the métro to the **place de la République** (3rd/Métro République). You can start your day at one of the many cafés around the square. Rue Faubourg du Temple comes off the square and if you follow it (northeast), you'll run into Quai de Valmy and Quai de Jemmapes along the Canal St-Martin.

It wasn't too long ago that guidebooks didn't even mention the 10th (other than perhaps a trip to Brasserie Flo). Today, this working-class area is increasingly popular with artists, making for an interesting mix. Boutiques, cafés, galleries and trendy restaurants seem to have multiplied overnight.

Winding through the 10th arrondissement on Paris's northeast side is the beautiful **Canal St-Martin**. The canal's bridges, foot-bridges and locks have been renovated. It's a great place to walk and relax.

The zinc bar at the 19th-century **Hôtel du Nord** (at 102 quai de Jemmapes) is a great place to take a break. *Info*: 10th/Métro J. Bonsergent or République. Tel. 01/40.40.78.78. Café open daily 9am-1:30pm, restaurant open daily noon-3pm and 8pm-midnight.

Canauxrama has two-hour cruises along the canal for €15.

Don't Miss ...

• a walk or boat tour along the Canal St-Martin
• delicious dining at a typical *brasserie*

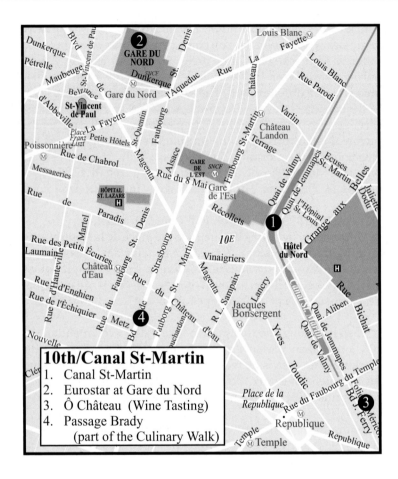

10th/Canal St-Martin
1. Canal St-Martin
2. Eurostar at Gare du Nord
3. Ô Château (Wine Tasting)
4. Passage Brady
   (part of the Culinary Walk)

Reservations can be made at Tel. 01/42.39.15.00. Boats depart from Port de l'Arsenal across from 50 blvd. de la Bastille (12th/Métro Bastille). www.canauxrama.com.

After you've spent a relaxing day along the canal, you can dine in this area at **Terminus Nord**. This large, bustling *brasserie* near the Gare du Nord is just so Parisian with its mahogany bar, polished wood and beveled glass. *Info*: 10th/Métro Gare du Nord. 23 rue de Dunkerque. Tel. 01/42.85.05.15. Moderate. Also a favorite in this area is **Brasserie Flo** serving Alsatian food in an 1886 *brasserie*, on a passageway in an area not frequented by tourists. *Info*: 10th/Métro Château d'Eau. 7 cour des Petites-

Écuries (enter from 63 rue du Fg-St-Denis). Tel. 01/47.70.13.59. Moderate.

After dinner, if you're interested in music, visit **New Morning**. This spartan music club is where you come to hear jazz, world music and folk. *Info*: 10th/Métro Château d'Eau. 7 rue des Petites-Écuries. Tel. 01/45.23.51.41. Open Mon-Sat 8pm-1:30am. Closed Sun.

Day 3 – On the Outskirts of Town: A Day in the 19th and 20th Arrondissements
Many visitors to Paris ignore areas of the city that are easily accessible, but a little off the beaten path. Today we'll head to the outskirts of town, to the 19th and 20th arrondissements. These diverse residential areas are home to the **Parc de la Villette** and the **Cimetière du Père-Lachaise**.

The futuristic **Parc de La Villette** is more than just a park. It features gardens and paths, but also has modern sculptures and bizarre park benches. A great place for kids. For years, this was the site of the city's slaughterhouses.

Don't Miss ...

• the futuristic **Parc de la Villette**
• the **Cimetière du Père-Lachaise**, the eternal home to an incredible list of people

Start your day by heading to the Métro Porte de Pantin. Here, you'll find the **Musée de la Musique**. Located in the **Cité de la Musique** (the $120 million stone-and-glass part of the Parc de la Villette), this museum features over 4,000 musical instruments from Baroque Italy to present-day France. You'll be given a headset (available in English). As you stroll through the museum, every time you approach an exhibit, the headset begins to play the music of that instrument. Very entertaining for kids and adults. *Info*: 19th/ Métro Porte de Pantin. 221 avenue Jean-Jaurès. Tel. 01/44.84.44.84. Open Tue-Sat noon-6pm, Sun 10am-6pm. Closed Mon. Admission: €8, under 18 free. www.cite-musique.fr.

If you're not a music aficionado, you can instead head to the Métro Porte de La Villette to visit the **Cité des Sciences et de**

l'Industrie (City of Science and Industry). This huge and spectacular museum is dedicated to science and industry, including **La Géode** (geodesic dome), a planetarium, aquarium, a submarine and much more. *Info*: 19th/Métro Porte de La Villette. At the northern edge of the city in the Parc de La Villette. 30 avenue Corentine-Cariou. Tel. 01/40.05.70.00. Open Tue-Sat 10am-6pm, Sun 10am-7pm. Closed Mon. Admission: €11, €9 ages 7-25, under 7 free. www.cite-sciences.fr.

Both attractions have places where you can have lunch.

In the afternoon, you should head to Métro Père-Lachaise and the **Cimetière du Père-Lachaise**.

In 1626, the Jesuits opened a retreat for retired priests on this site. Father (Père) Lachaise, Louis XIV's confessor, visited here often. The Jesuits were expelled in 1763 and the city bought the property (all 110 acres) and converted it into a cemetery. It's the largest cemetery in Paris and is the eternal home to an incredible list of people, including Maria Callas, Chopin, Oscar Wilde, Balzaç, Bellini, Proust, Modigliani, Gertrude Stein and Edith Piaf. Oh yeah, Jim Morrison of The Doors is buried here, too (as you can tell by the hordes of fans near his grave, which has become a pilgrimage for his admirers). The graves range from simple, unadorned headstones to elaborate monuments and chapels.

Despite the fact that you're wandering in a cemetery, the grounds are quite beautiful and there are over 3,000 trees here. Each family is responsible for the upkeep of the family plot, and some are in  extreme states of disrepair. There's a new 30-year-lease policy in place, so if the family doesn't renew the lease, the remains can be removed. It's believed that Jim Morrison's lease will never expire, much to the dismay of families who have their plots nearby.

If you enter the cemetery from the back off of rue des Rondeaux, you'll find the **Jardin du Souvenir**, with a series of stark, heart-wrenching memorials and tombstones dedicated to those who died in military combat or concentration camps during World War II.

Info: 20th/Métro Père-Lachaise. Enter off the boulevard de Menilmontant. Open daily Mon-Fri 8am-6pm, Sat 8:30am-6pm, and Sun 9am-6pm. Closes at 5:30pm Nov-early Mar. Free maps available at the main entrance when a guard is on duty. Admission: Free. See Major Sights (East) Map.

I have two suggestions for you for dinner in this area. "Foodies" love **La Cave Gourmande**, and I had one of the best meals of my life here. *Info*: 19th/Métro Danube or Botzaris. 10 rue du Général-Brunet. Tel. 01/40.40.03.30. Closed Sat, Sun & part of Aug. Moderate-Expensive. If you're looking for something a little less fancy, try **La Boulangerie**, a classic French bistro located in a former bakery in the increasingly trendy Ménilmontant area near Père-Lachaise cemetery. *Info*: 20th/Métro Ménilmontant. 15 rue des Panoyaux. Tel. 01/43.58.45.45. Closed Sat (lunch) & Sun. Moderate.

Day 4 – A Day in Montparnasse
Montparnasse is centered around the lively boulevard Montparnasse (once the center of Paris's avant-garde scene). Although this area is primarily residential, there's plenty to keep you busy for a day.

To start your day, you can head to the **Tour Montparnasse** (Montparnasse Tower). This unfortunate 1970s black glass tower that dominates its Left Bank neighbors has an observation deck. Take the elevator to the 56th floor and then steps to the roof. There was such outrage after this tower was built that an ordinance was

Don't Miss ...

- the view of Paris from the **Tour Montparnasse**
- historic **cafés**
- contemporary art at the **Fondation Cartier**

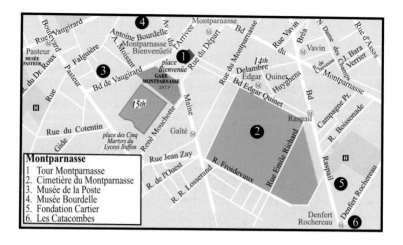

passed prohibiting further towers in the city center. The best thing about the great view is that you can't see this tower! *Info*: 15th/Métro Montparnasse-Bienvenüe. Open daily Apr-Sep 9:30am-11:30pm, Oct-Mar 9:30am-10:30pm. Last ascension a half-hour before closing. Admission: €9.

After visiting the tower, you might want to head to the nearby **Cimetière du Montparnasse**. This quiet but somewhat messy cemetery is the "permanent home" of Samuel Beckett, Jean-Paul Sartre, Simone de Beauvoir and other celebrities of the past. *Info*: 14th/Métro Edgar Quinet. Enter on either rue Froidevaux or boulevard Edgar Quinet off of boulevard Raspail. Open daily 9am-5:30pm. Admission: Free.

You can now head to the **Musée de la Poste** (Postal Museum), devoted to French and international philately (stamp collections). *Info*: 15th/Métro Pasteur or Montparnasse-Bienvenüe. 34 boulevard de Vaugirard. Tel. 01/42.79.24.24. Open Mon-Sat 10am-6pm. Closed Sun. Admission: €5, under 18 free. www.museedelaposte.fr.

If you're not interested in stamps but are interested in sculpture, head to the **Musée Bourdelle**. Bourdelle was a student of Rodin. Bourdelle's famous 21 studies of Beethoven are housed here. *Info*: 15th/Métro Montparnasse-Bienvenüe or Falguière. 16-18 rue

Antoine Bourdelle. Tel. 01/49.54.73.73. Open Tue-Sun 10am-6pm. Closed Mon. Admission: Permanent collection is free. €5 for exhibits.

For lunch, here are two choices on boulevard Montparnasse. **La Coupole** (*Info*: 14th/Métro Vavin. 102 boulevard du Montparnasse. Tel. 01/43.20.14.20. Moderate)

has been a Montparnasse institution since the days of Picasso. This noisy *brasserie* is known for its oysters. **La Closerie des Lilas** (*Info*: 14th/ Métro Raspail or Vavin. 171 boulevard du Montparnasse. Tel. 01/40.51.34.50. Moderate-Expensive) is a historic café where Lenin and Trotsky and many other famous people hung out. There's a terrace, piano bar, *brasserie* and restaurant.

In the afternoon, head to **Fondation Cartier**. This contemporary art-and-photography museum is housed in an incredible glass building. *Info*: 14th/Métro Raspail. 261 boulevard Raspail. Tel. 01/42.18.56.50. Open Tue-Sun noon-8pm. Closed Mon. Admission: €7.

For dinner, make the trip to **Le Severo** for a truly Parisian experience. The chef used to be a butcher and the beef here is fantastic. Make the trip just for the fries! The wine blackboard fills a whole wall of this bistro. *Info*: 14th/Métro Alésia. 8 rue des Plantes. Tel. 01/45.40.40.91. Closed Sat (dinner) and Sun. Moderate.

Day 5 – No Tourist Day

You're not going to see a lot of other tourists on this day plan, and that can be a good thing! We'll visit part of the 5th, 12th, and 13th arrondissements on this day. The part of the 5th that we'll be visiting is filled with diverse sights. The 12th is home to the Gare de Lyon train station. This primarily residential area is bordered on the east by the Bois de Vincennes, a beautiful park. The 13th is a residential area, home to Chinatown (13 square blocks around the Tolbiac métro stop) and the grand National Library.

Don't Miss ...

• the **Bibliothèque Nationale de France,** France's grand National Library
• lunch at the stunning **Le Train Bleu**
• relaxing in the **Jardin des Plantes**

Begin your day by heading on the métro to the Bibliothèque stop.

The colossal, wedge-shaped **MK2 Bibliothèque** at 128/162 Ave. de France, in front of the Bibliothèque National de France, has a cinema with 14 screens, a bar and several restaurants. This is a good place to have breakfast.

You'll now head over to the **Bibliothèque Nationale de France.** France's National Library, the pet project of former president François Mitterand, has four towers that were designed to represent open books (it's a library, after all). It has a wonderful bookstore, and there's a peaceful sunken courtyard. If you're not a scholar, you'll probably just want to take a look at the immense exterior and down into the courtyard garden. *Info*: 13th/Métro Bibliothèque. quai François-Mauriac. Tel. 01/53.79.59.59. Open Tue-Sat 10am-8pm, Sun noon-7pm. Closed Mon. Admission: €3.50 (to reading rooms). www.bnf.fr.

The National Library is on the same métro line (#14) as the **Gare de Lyon** train station (only a few stops away). Why don't you

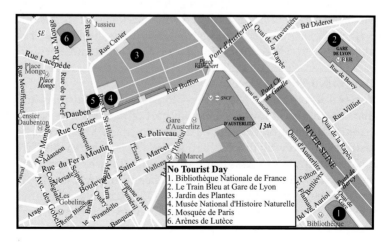

No Tourist Day
1. Bibliothèque Nationale de France
2. Le Train Bleu at Gare de Lyon
3. Jardin des Plantes
4. Musée National d'Histoire Naturelle
5. Mosquée de Paris
6. Arènes de Lutèce

head here for lunch? Lunch at a train station? Forget all the food you've eaten in train stations. It's delicious at **Le Train Bleu**. But you don't really come for the food anyway because the setting, with its murals of the French-speaking world, is spectacular. A great place to have a drink.

In the afternoon, you can visit one of the great parks of Paris and work off your lunch. Take the métro to the Jussieu or Monge stops. The **Jardin des Plantes** is a quiet park not frequented by many travelers. It's especially known for its herb garden. The zoo here (the **Ménagerie**) is one of the oldest in the world. *Info*: 5th/ Métro Jussieu or Monge. Off of the Quai St-Bernard, west of Gare d'Austerlitz. Tel. 01/40.79.30.00. Open daily 8am-5:30pm. Zoo open daily 9am-5pm. Admission: Free (gardens), €7 (zoo).

Also at the park is the **Musée National d'Histoire Naturelle** (National Museum of Natural History). Visit the Gallery of the Evolution of Man and exhibits on everything from entomology (the study of insects) to paleontology (the study of dinosaurs). You'll be greeted by a huge whale skeleton. (You may want to skip the skeletons of fetuses and Siamese twins.) *Info*: 5th/Métro Jussieu. 57 rue Cuvier. Tel. 01/40.79.30.00. Open 10am-5pm. Closed Tue. Admission: €7, €5 ages 4-16 and over 60, under 4 free.

Nearby is the **Mosquée de Paris**, modeled after the Alhambra in Spain. This pink mosque was built in the 1920s as a tribute to Muslims from North Africa who supported France in World War I. It's the spiritual center for Muslims in Paris. There's a tea room, a school, and Turkish baths on the premises. *Info*: 5th/Métro Monge. 2b place du Puits-de-l'Ermite. Tel. 01/45.35.97.33. Open 9am-noon and 2pm-8pm. Closed Fridays and Islamic holidays. Admission: €3.

ALTERNATIVE PLAN

While most of Paris is devoid of tall skyscrapers, **La Défense** is home to many modern, interesting office buildings. The crown jewel is the huge **Grande Arche de La Défense**, a modern arch aligned with the (tiny, by comparison) Arc de Triomphe. You could fit Notre-Dame under it. Glass tube elevators can take you to the top for 7€. *Info*: Métro Grande Arche de La Défense. Parvis de La Défense. Tel. 01/49.07.27.57. Open daily.

Not far from here is another sight that you can just pop into. The **Arènes de Lutèce** is a 1st-century Roman arena in the midst of Paris. In a word, unique. And, you won't find many tourists here, either. *Info*: 5th/Métro Monge. rue Monge and rue de Navarre. Open daily dawn to dusk. Admission: Free.

You can dine at **Le Petit Marguery**, a 1930s bistro featuring game dishes and known for its good service. It's a safe bet that there won't be tourists at the next table. *Info*: 13th/Métro Gobelins. 9 boulevard de Port-Royal. Tel. 01/43.31.58.59. Closed Sun, Mon & Aug. Moderate.

Day 6 – Exploring Quirky Paris

Paris has some of the world's best-known sights. It also has some of the oddest. So here are your choices, broken down into categories: Crap, Dead Stuff, Medicine and Animals. Enjoy!.

Crap:

Les Egouts (The Sewers)

Why would you want to visit the sewers of Paris? Many do, despite the smell (especially bad in summer). You can visit the huge underground passages in the bowels of the city (no pun intended), a museum, and view a film. *Info*: 7th/Métro Alma-Marceau. Pont de l'Alma (opposite 93 quai d'Orsay). Tel. 01/53.68.27.81. Open 11am-4pm (May-Sep until 5pm). Closed Thu, Fri and most of Jan. Admission: €4, under 5 free. See Eiffel Tower Area Map.

Dead Stuff:
Les Catacombes
Grim, strange and claustro-
phobic. Beginning in the late
1700s, six million people were
deposited in what used to be
stone quarries. It gets even
creepier. The bones are ar-
ranged in patterns. Not for
everyone. *Info*: 14th/Métro

Denfert-Rochereau. 1 place Denfert-Rochereau. Tel. 01/
43.22.47.63. Open Tue-Sun 2pm-4pm. Closed Mon. Admission:
€6.50, under 14 free. See Montparnasse Map.

Chapelle Notre-Dame de la Médaille Miraculeuse (Chapel of
Our Lady of the Miraculous Medal)
Catherine Labouré was a young nun when she claimed that the
Virgin Mary, dressed in a white silk dress, visited her (four times
in 1827) to deliver a design for a holy medal. Go figure! Catherine's
body is here in a glass cage. The spot where the Virgin Mary is
said to have sat during her visits is a place of veneration. You can
buy a rosary or medal in the courtyard (they actually have a
machine that dispenses these souvenirs). Another glass cage
holds the body of St. Louise de Marillac (one of the founders of the
Daughters of Charity). St. Louise is still wearing her habit. *Info*:
7th/Métro Sèvres-Babylone. 140 rue du Bac. Open daily 7:45am-
1pm and 2:30pm-7pm. Admission: Free.

Around the corner is **La Congrégation de la Mission** (Congregation
of the Mission). Here, the waxed corpse of St. Vincent de Paul
(known for his charity) is found in an ornate glass-and-silver casket
above the main altar. If you like this sort of macabre stuff, you can
climb the stairs and get a close-up view of his body. *Info*: 7th/Métro
Sèvres-Babylone. 95 rue de Sèvres. Open daily. Admission: Free.
See Eiffel Tower Area Map.

Medicine:
Musée d'Histoire de la Médecine (Museum of Medical History)
Yikes! You can see implements used for skull drilling in this 100-
year-old museum dedicated to medical history. The implements

used to perform Napoléon's autopsy are here, too. *Info*: 6th/Métro Odéon. 12 rue de l'Ecole de Médecine. In the René Descartes University (second floor). Tel. 01/40.46.16.93. Open Oct-July 15 2pm-5:30pm except Thu and Sun, July 15-Sep 2pm-5:30pm except Sat and Sun. Admission: €4. See Left Bank Map.

Musée Orfila (Anatomy Museum)
Formaldehyde jars with Siamese twins and deformed body parts, wax models of anuses and skinned faces, and the mummified bodies of a whole family are some of the horrid exhibits that greet you in the eighth-floor lobby of this university. Fun! *Info*: 6th/ Métro St-Germain-des-Prés. 45 rue des Sts-Pères. (in the René Descartes Université). Tel. 01/42.86.22.59. Open hours vary, usually Tue and Thu 2pm-5pm. Admission: Free. See Left Bank Map.

Musée de l'Assistance Publique - Hôpitaux de Paris (Museum of Public Assistance and Hospitals)
Interested in exhibits on infanticide or "historic" blood-covered uniforms? If so, this museum is right up your alley! The 17th-century mansion used to be a pharmacy. *Info*: 5th/Métro Maubert-Mutualité. 47 quai de la Tournelle. Open Tue-Sun 10am-6pm. Closed Mon and Aug. Tel. 01/40.27.50.05. Admission: €4, under 13 free. Free first Sun of the month. See Left Bank Map.

Animals:
For the truly adventurous, you can head out of Paris to one of these sights:

Musée Fragonard d'Alfort (Veterinary Museum)
Ugh! Animal skeletons, skinned cats, a camel's stomach and a partially flayed 200-year-old horse and its rider are just some of the rather grim exhibits at this veterinary school's museum. *Info:* Métro Alfort - École Vétérinaire. In the suburb of Maisons-Alfort/Métro Alfort-École Vétérinaire. Located in the National Veterinary School. Tel. 01/43.96.71.72 (call ahead, as times vary). Open Tue and Wed 2pm-5pm and Sat-Sun 10am-5pm. Closed Aug. Admission: €3.50.

Cimetière des Chiens (Dog Cemetery)
The French love their dogs (and cats) so much that they have an entire cemetery with some elaborate memorials to countless poodles and even Rin Tin Tin. How totally French! *Info*: In the Asnières-sur-Siene suburb/Métro Mairie de Clichy (line 13). A 15-minute walk from métro on rue Martre, left at end of the bridge Pont de Clichy. Located along the river. 4 Pont de Clichy (on the river). Tel. 01/40.86.21.11. Open Mar-Oct 10am-6pm, Nov-Feb 10am-4:30pm. Closed Mon and Tue. Admission: €3.

For dinner, try the quirky **Roger La Grenouille,** where you may find yourself wearing one of the many hats hanging on the wall while dining. *Info*: 6th/Métro Odéon. 26 rue des Grands-Augustins. Tel. 01/56.24.24.34. Closed Sun. Moderate.

Another option is **Nos Ancêtres les Gaulois** where the waiters are humorously rude. It's not so much dining as an experience. *Info*: 4th/Métro Pont Marie. 39 rue Saint-Louis-en-l'Île. Tel. 01/46.33.66.07. Moderate.

Day 7. Excursion Day: Vaux-le-Vicomte or Fontainebleau
We'll venture out of Paris today to see some opulent sights at **Vaux-le-Vicomte**.

Trains depart from Gare de Lyon to Melun (the same trains that run to Fontainebleau). Vaux-le-Vicomte is 13 miles north of Fontainebleau. It's a 4-mile taxi ride from the train station at Melun (€15), or the Chateaubus shuttle (weekends and holidays only, €7 roundtrip).

Nicolas Fouquet, the finance minister to France in the mid-1600s, built this beautiful *château*. It's said that when Louis XIV visited, he soon had the finance minister arrested and then stole his art treasures. Louis XIV then used the planners of this *château* to build Versailles (on a larger scale). The garden is filled with statues, fountains and waterfalls, and is the site of special events including impressive candlelight tours. A calendar of these special events is found at www.vaux-le-vicomte.com. *Info*: Tel. 01/64.14.41.90. Open daily 10am-6pm from Easter to mid-Nov. Admission: €12.50.

Another opulent destination is **Fontainebleau**.

Trains depart Gare de Lyon. A 50-60 minute trip. €15 round-trip. The palace is 1-1/2 miles from the train station. A bus runs every 15-30 minutes from the station (€2). Tickets including train, bus fare and admission cost €20 and are available at Gare de Lyon.

The French monarchy used this as a resort and for hunting in its forest. Like Versailles, it's a study in excess, but it's not as grand as Versailles. Highlights include the elegant ballroom, the golden Throne Room, the elaborate Louis XV staircase and the Gallery of François I. The gardens are also not as grand as Versailles, but certainly beautiful to stroll in. *Info*: Tel. 01/60.71.50.70. Château: Open Wed-Mon 9:30am-5pm (Jun-Sep until 6pm). Closed Tue. Admission: €6, under 18 free. www.musee-chateau-fontainebleau.fr.

When you return to Paris, have a leisurely dinner at **Bofinger**, a beautiful glass-roofed brasserie with lots of stained glass and brass, located between the place des Vosges and the place de la Bastille. *Info*: 4th/Métro Bastille. 5 rue de la Bastille. Tel. 01/42.72.87.82. Open daily until 1 am. Moderate.

Across the street and less expensive is **Le Petit Bofinger**, 6 rue de la Bastille. Tel. 01/42.72.05.23.

6. GREAT WALKS IN PARIS

The real reason the French are thin ...

The French have two-hour lunches with lots of wine and dinners that include dishes smothered with delicious cream sauces, even more wine and sinful desserts. So why are they so thin?

It's simple: **They walk everywhere.** To the market, to the cinema and yes, to the bistro. Now, you too can travel to Paris, eat and drink all you want and (hopefully!) not gain a pound. All you have to do is venture out on the walks in this chapter.

Go ahead, eat like the French. Then, refer to this chapter and get your exercise – and see the best Paris has to offer!

For in-depth details of the sights covered here, see earlier chapters.

ISLANDS WALK

Approximate distance: two miles. **Highlights:** Notre-Dame, Ste-Chapelle and Île St-Louis.

Your walk begins by taking the métro to the Pont Neuf stop.

You'll be in front of **La Samaritaine** department store at 19 rue de la Monnaie (closed for renovations).

Head east along the Seine River.

Along the river on quai de la Mégisserie (between rue des Bourdonnais and place du Châtelet) you can wander through beautiful **plant stores** and **pet shops** (birds, puppies, fish, roosters, you name it) that spill out onto the sidewalks. You'll love this little strip of Paris.

When you reach **place du Châtelet**, take in the **Fountain of the Palms**. It was ordered by Napoléon to commemorate his victories in Egypt.

Turn to your right and cross the bridge.

The **Pont-au-Change** got its name because moneychangers used to have their booths on this bridge crossing the Seine River.

On the other side of the Pont-au-Change is the boulevard du Palais.

On the corner, look up and you'll see a fabulous 1334 Baroque **clock tower** (it still works), the first public clock in Paris. You're now on the **Île de la Cité**, an island in the Seine River.

Continue down the boulevard du Palais.

On your right is the entrance to the **Musée de la Conciergerie**, a 14th-century prison where over 2,600 people waited to have their heads chopped off, including Marie-Antoinette, during the French

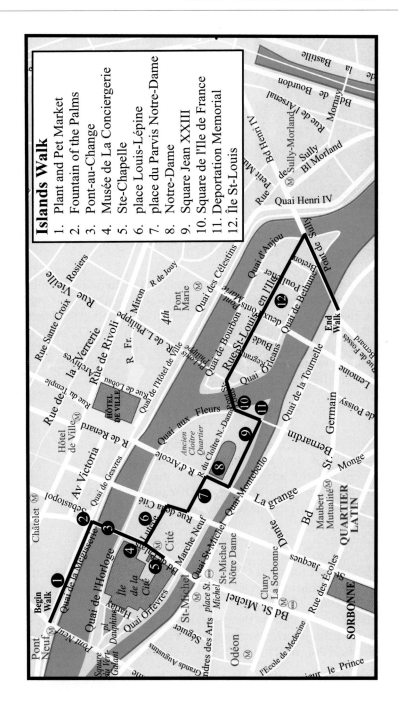

Islands Walk

1. Plant and Pet Market
2. Fountain of the Palms
3. Pont-au-Change
4. Musée de La Conciergerie
5. Ste-Chapelle
6. place Louis-Lépine
7. place du Parvis Notre-Dame
8. Notre-Dame
9. Square Jean XXIII
10. Square de l'Ile de France
11. Deportation Memorial
12. Île St-Louis

revolution's "Reign of Terror." If you have limited time, skip this museum and head down the street.

The Gothic palace that houses this museum along with the massive **Palais de Justice** were once part of the Palais de la Cité, the home of French kings. Today, it's home to the city's courts of law. You can watch the courts in session and view its beautiful interior for free. Closed on Sunday.

As you pass the gates to the palace, on your right, you'll see the entrance to our next stop.

If it's a sunny day, you cannot miss **la Ste-Chapelle**. You'll be dazzled by nearly 6,600 square feet of stained glass at this Gothic masterpiece. The walls are almost entirely stained glass. Fifteen windows depict biblical scenes from the Garden of Eden to the Apocalypse (the large rose window). The chapel was built in 1246 to house what some believe to be the Crown of Thorns, a nail from the crucifixion and other relics.

Cross the boulevard du Palais to rue de Lutèce.

Soon you'll see, to your left, the curvy, Art Nouveau Cité métro stop. You're now in the **place Louis-Lépine**. To your left is the lovely **Marché aux Fleurs** (flower market). On Sundays, the market becomes the **Marché aux Oiseaux** (bird market) where all types of birds, supplies and cages are sold.

Continue on and turn right at rue de la Cité.

Head down rue de la Cité to **place du Parvis Notre-Dame** (the square in front of Notre-Dame). It's recently been renamed Parvis Notre-Dame/place Jean-Paul-II. It's the center of all of France. The bronze plaque on the ground outside the cathedral is "Point Zéro" from which all distances in France are measured. You'll also find the entry to the **Crypte Archéologique** here with ruins of Roman Paris. Head into **Notre-Dame** and admire this incredible structure.

As you exit the cathedral (with the cathedral to your back) head left and then make a left turn before the bridge.

Stroll through **Square Jean XXIII** along the river. Behind the cathedral is the lovely **Square de l'Île de France**. Here you'll notice the "flying buttresses" that support Notre-Dame. From these squares, take in the beauty of Paris along the Seine River.

Directly behind the cathedral, cross the street (quai Archevêché) and head through the gate.

You'll now enter the **Mémorial des Martyrs Français de la Déportation de 1945** (Deportation Memorial). It will take you only a short time to walk through this free memorial built in honor of the more than 30,000 citizens who were placed on boats at this spot for deportation to concentration camps. You descend steps and become surrounded by walls. Single-file, you enter a chamber. A hallway is covered with 200,000 crystals (one for each French citizen who died). At the far end of the hall is the eternal flame of hope. Don't miss this memorial. It's both moving and disturbing.

As you leave the memorial, exit out the gate, turn right on quai Archevêché. Head to the pedestrian bridge. Take a right onto the bridge.

You are now on the **Pont St-Louis**. There almost always are street musicians playing jazz to a crowd of onlookers.

Continue across this bridge to the Île St-Louis.

The **Île St-Louis** is a residential island within the city, often swamped with tourists during high season. The vast majority of the buildings on this island date back to the 1600s, making for a beautiful place to stroll, especially the small side streets. There are interesting shops and several good restaurants.

The Best of Île St-Louis

- No. 78: **Boulangerie St-Louis**. A great bakery.
- No. 69: **Mon Vieil Ami**. Popular and trendy bistro.
- No. 51: **Kabrousse**. A great photo op as the flowers spill out onto the sidewalk.
- No. 31: **Berthillon**. The best-known ice-cream shop in Paris.
- No. 19: **Eglise St-Louis-en-l'Île**. Visit the beautiful ornate interior of this church.

After you cross the bridge you'll be on the narrow **rue St-Louis-en-l'Île**, one of the most beautiful streets in all of Paris.

At the end of the street, turn right and cross the bridge.

This bridge (**Pont Sully**) dates back to 1874 and is actually two independent steel bridges that extend from the Île St-Louis to either side of the river. You're now on the Left Bank and can continue down the famous boulevard St-Germain-des-Prés.

You can head back to your hotel from any number of métro stops along the boulevard St-Germain-des-Prés.

LEFT BANK WALK

Approximate distance: two-and-a-half miles. **Highlights:** Musée Maillol, St-Germain-des-Prés, and the Jardin du Luxembourg. Musée Maillol is closed on Tuesday.

Take the métro to the rue du Bac stop.

When you get out of the métro, you'll be at the crossroads of rue du Bac, boulevard Raspail and boulevard St-Germain-des-Prés. On the corner is a typical Parisian café, the **Café St-Germain**. Why don't you start by having coffee and a croissant here? If you order *un café*, you'll get a small cup of very strong black coffee. If you'd like a larger cup of coffee with steamed milk, ask for *un crème*.

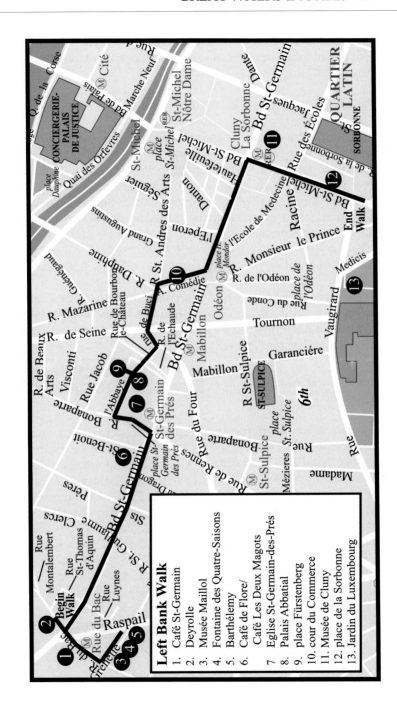

Left Bank Walk
1. Café St-Germain
2. Deyrolle
3. Musée Maillol
4. Fontaine des Quatre-Saisons
5. Barthélemy
6. Café de Flore/
   Café Les Deux Magots
7. Eglise St-Germain-des-Prés
8. Palais Abbatial
9. place Fürstenberg
10. cour du Commerce
11. Musée de Cluny
12. place de la Sorbonne
13. Jardin du Luxembourg

After you've had your wonderful Parisian coffee, you're going to visit one of the most interesting, if not the most bizarre, shops in Paris.

Cross rue Raspail and boulevard St-Germain-des-Prés to rue du Bac.

At 46 rue du Bac you'll find **Deyrolle**, a taxidermy shop "stuffed" with everything from snakes to baby elephants to zebras. Also on display are collections of butterflies, shells and minerals from all over the world. Kids seem to love this place. You have to go upstairs! The shop also sells planters, clothes and other household items (some modeled on the stuffed animals). Very quirky! It's closed on Sunday.

Head back toward the café and up rue de Bac in the opposite direction.

On this short block, you'll find everything from a butcher shop to a fish shop, and an attractive antique shop called **Magnolia**. Notice that horse head above the butcher shop on your left? That means that the store still sells horse meat.

When you get to rue de Grenelle, make a left.

Two Great Restaurants

As you head down rue de Grenelle, you can stop at the **Musée Maillol** (Fondation Dina Vierny-Musée Maillol) at 61. The works of Aristide Maillol, a contemporary of Matisse, are here, along with rare sketches by Picasso, Cézanne, Degas and other 20th-century artists. The museum also features important exhibits. It opens at 11am and is closed on Tuesday.

Next to the museum is the **Fontaine des Quatre-Saisons**,

Two famous chefs have opened restaurants in this area. At 44 rue du Bac, Pierre Gagnaire transformed a 1912 fish house into **Gaya**. Tel. 01/45.44.73.73. Across the street, in the Hôtel Pont Royal at 5 rue de Montalembert, is the famous chef Joël Robuchon's **L'Atelier de Joël Robuchon** where "foodies" sit at the counter sampling innovative dishes. Tel. 01/42.22.56.56.

completed in 1745. It's decorated with figures representing the four seasons (and a few cherubs thrown in for good measure).

Cheese is like gold to the French. Charles de Gaulle is reported to have said, "How can anyone govern a nation that has 246 different kinds of cheese?" At number 51 is **Barthélemy**, a small, popular cheese shop. You'll know when you're getting close as you'll be able to smell it. When you walk in, you're overtaken by the intense smell of some of the best cheeses available in France. Closed Sunday and Monday.

Let's backtrack to the café (down rue de Grenelle to rue du Bac). Turn right onto boulevard St-Germain-des-Prés. Walk down the left side of this famous boulevard.

At 218 is **Madeleine Gely**, a shop that's been making handmade umbrellas since 1834.

You have not experienced Paris unless you visit one of its many cafés. **Café de Flore** is at 172 boulevard St-Germain-des-Prés. Just a few steps away is **Café Les Deux Magots** at 6 place St-Germain-des-Prés. Great people-watching at both of these famous cafés.

In between Café Les Deux Magots and Café de Flore is **La Hune**, at 170 boulevard St-Germain, This incredible bookstore is packed until midnight with Parisian and foreign "intellectuals." There's an extensive architecture-and-art section upstairs.

Take a left at place St-Germain-des-Prés.

Stop into the **Eglise St-Germain-des-Prés**. This church dates back to the 6th century. A Gothic choir, 19th-century spire and Romanesque paintings all attest to its long history.

As you exit the church, head right and then turn right onto rue de l'Abbaye.

On the right side of rue de l'Abbaye is the rose-colored 17th-century **Palais Abbatial**.

Take a left into place Fürstenberg.

At the center of **place Fürstenberg** is a white-globed lamppost. Look familiar? This scenic square has been seen in many films. It's often filled with street musicians, some of them surprisingly good.

Head back to rue de l'Abbaye and continue down the street which turns into rue de Bourbon-le-Château.

On the corner is a wonderful wine shop, **La Dernière Goutte**.

Take a left on the attractive rue de Buci.

On rue de Buci, you'll pass along small cafés and interesting shops on a mostly pedestrian street. At the intersection of rue de Buci and rue St-André-des-Arts, you'll find a typical French outdoor market at certain times of the day.

Rue de Buci turns into rue St-André-des-Arts. Take a right at 61.

The **cour du Commerce** is a cobblestone alleyway off of la rue St-André-des-Arts, which is lined with wonderful shops and res-

taurants. Benjamin Franklin is said to have frequented **Procope**, the oldest *brasserie* in Paris.

At the end of the passageway, turn left and you'll be back on boulevard St-Germain. Continue on this street and take a right onto boulevard St-Michel.

On your left at the intersection is the **Musée de Cluny** (Musée National du Moyen Age/Thermes de Cluny) at 6 place Paul-

Painlevé. The building that houses this museum (the **Hôtel de Cluny**) has had many lives. It's been a Roman bathhouse in the 3rd century (you can still visit the ruins downstairs), a mansion for a religious abbot in the 15th century, a royal residence, and, since 1844, a museum. Don't miss the chapel on the second floor. It's a splendid example of flamboyant Gothic architecture.

If you're interested in medieval arts and crafts, you must visit this museum. Chalices, manuscripts, crosses, vestments, carvings, sculptures and the acclaimed Lady and the Unicorn tapestries are all here. You enter through the cobblestoned **Cour d'Honneur** (Court of Honor), surrounded by the Gothic building with its gargoyles and turrets. Even if you don't visit the museum, you can visit the beautiful medieval garden.

Continue down the boulevard St-Michel.

On your left, you'll see the beautiful fountains in the **place de la Sorbonne**. This is the site of one of the most famous universities in the world. Take a break here at one of the many cafés and soak in the college ambience.

Return to boulevard St-Michel and continue in the same direction.

On your right, you'll soon see the black-and-gold fence surrounding the huge **Jardin du Luxembourg** (Luxembourg Gardens), where you'll end your walk. These formal French gardens are referred to as the heart of the Left Bank. Also here is the **Palais du Luxembourg** (Luxembourg Palace), the home of the French Senate, and the **Musée du Luxembourg** (Luxembourg Museum), featuring temporary exhibitions of some of the big names in the history of art.

You can return to the intersection of boulevard St-Michel and boulevard St-Germain-des-Prés and take the Cluny-La Sorbonne métro back to your hotel.

MARAIS WALK

Approximate distance: two miles. **Highlights:** Musée Picasso, place des Vosges, and Centre Pompidou.

Take the métro to the St-Paul stop. When you get out of the métro, you'll be on rue St-Antoine.

Start walking (east) on the right side of rue St-Antoine until you reach 101, the **Eglise St-Paul-St-Louis**. Stop into this Baroque church with its huge dome dating back to the 1600s. Take a look at the Delacroix painting *Christ on the Mount of Olives* and the shell-shaped holy-water fonts.

Continue on rue St-Antoine until you reach rue St-Paul. Turn right on rue St-Paul and then turn right at 23/25/27 rue St-Paul.

You're now in the **Village St-Paul**, an attractive passageway with interesting stores that's known for its antique shops.

Head back to the intersection of rue St-Paul and rue St-Antoine. Take a right, cross the street at the next crosswalk, and walk to 62 rue St-Antoine.

Look at the exterior of the **Hôtel Sully**, a mansion in the French Renaissance style and housing **Caisse Nationale des Monuments Historiques**, the headquarters for administering France's historic monuments. Walk into the courtyard and beautiful garden.

Continue down rue St-Antoine and make a left at rue de Birague.

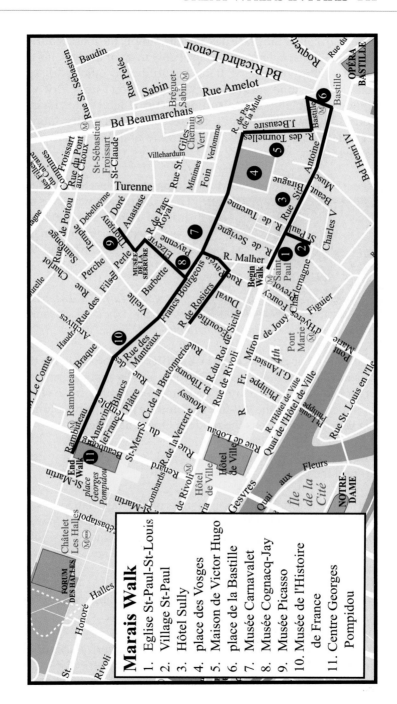

Marais Walk

1. Eglise St-Paul-St-Louis
2. Village St-Paul
3. Hôtel Sully
4. place des Vosges
5. Maison de Victor Hugo
6. place de la Bastille
7. Musée Carnavalet
8. Musée Cognacq-Jay
9. Musée Picasso
10. Musée de l'Histoire de France
11. Centre Georges Pompidou

You'll now enter the **place des Vosges**, simply the most beautiful square in Paris, in France, and probably in all of Europe. It's the oldest square in the city. It's a beautiful and quiet park surrounded by stone and red-brick houses. Don't miss it! If you want, you can stop at **Maison de Victor Hugo** (Victor Hugo's house), 6 place des Vosges, to view this 19th-century literary legend's home (he wrote *Les Miserables* and *The Hunchback of Notre Dame*).

Need a break? Stop in at **Ma Bourgogne,** 19 place des Vosges.

This café/restaurant serves traditional Parisian cuisine and specializes in roast chicken. It's a great place for coffee. Tel. 01/42.78.44.64.

After your break, it's back to rue St-Antoine. Take a left. At the end of rue St-Antoine is a huge traffic roundabout.

You're now at the **place de la Bastille**. The notorious Bastille prison was torn down over 200 years ago by mobs during the French Revolution. Today, it's a roundabout traffic circle where cars speed around the 170-foot **Colonne de Julliet** (July Column). On the opposite side is the modern **Opéra Bastille**.

This is another opportunity for a break as there are many cafés around the place de la Bastille.

On nearby rue Richard Lenoir (a street off the traffic circle, to your left as you're looking at the **July Column**), the outdoor **Marché Bastille** market is held every Thursday and Sunday. It's filled with colorful vendors selling everything from stinky cheese to African masks.

At the end of rue St-Antoine, turn left and walk a short distance and then turn left on rue de la Bastille.

At 5 rue de la Bastille is **Bofinger**, a beautiful glass-roofed *brasserie*, with lots of stained glass and brass. It's the oldest Alsatian *brasserie* in Paris and still serves traditional dishes like *choucroute* (sauerkraut) and large platters of shellfish. Tel. 01/ 42.72.87.82. Across the street and less expensive is **Le Petit Bofinger**. Tel. 01/42.72.05.23.

Turn right from rue de la Bastille onto rue des Tournelles.

At number 6 is the cozy restaurant **Gaspard de la Nuit**, Tel 01/ 42.77.90.53. You'll pass another well-known restaurant at 38 rue des Tournelles. **Bistrot de l'Oulette** (formerly Baracane) is an intimate, moderately priced restaurant featuring the specialties of Southwest France. Tel. 01/42.71.43.33, Closed Saturday (lunch) and Sunday. On the left side of the street (between the two restaurants) at number 21 is the **Synagogue des Tournelles**. Gustave Eiffel (who designed the extraordinary tower that bears his name) was the engineer of the metal structure of this synagogue.

Turn left at rue du Pas-de-la-Mule.

At 6 rue du Pas-de-la-Mule you'll find the fascinating **Instruments Musicaux Anciens**. This curious little place, once a butcher shop, is jammed with musical instruments, from accordions to zithers. Stop in if it's open (most afternoons).

Continue down rue du Pas-de-la-Mule through the arcades of the place des Vosges. This street turns into the rue des Francs-Bourgeois.

At the corner of rue des Francs-Bourgeois and rue de Sévigné is the often-overlooked **Musée Carnavalet**. You'll find antiques, portraits and artifacts dating back to the late 1700s in this free museum. The section on the French Revolution with its guillotines is interesting, as is

Detour

Off of rue des Francs-Bourgeois, you can turn left down rue Pavée and then right onto rue des Rosiers and you find yourself in the heart of Jewish Paris. Rue des Rosiers is a great place to get a falafel sandwich and to view shop windows filled with Jewish artifacts. You'll need to retrace your steps back to rue des Francs-Bourgeois.

the royal bedroom. There are exhibits across the courtyard at the **Hôtel le Peletier de St-Fargeau**. It's closed on Monday.

Continue on rue des Francs-Bourgeois and make a right on rue Elzévir.

You'll pass the **Musée Cognacq-Jay** at 8 rue Elzévir. This free museum houses the 18th-century art and furniture collection of the founder of La Samaritaine department store. Works by Rembrandt, Fragonard, Boucher and others are here in this quiet museum housed in the **Hôtel Donon**, an elegant mansion. It's closed on Monday.

Continue down rue Elzévir. It intersects with rue de Thorigny.

At 5 rue de Thorigny, you'll find the **Musée Picasso** (don't worry; if you're getting lost, there are signs directing you to the museum). This houses the world's largest collection of the works of Picasso in a 17th-century mansion. It's closed on Tuesday.

Head back to rue des Francs-Bourgeois.

At 60 rue des Francs-Bourgeois, you'll find the **Musée de l'Histoire de France/Musée des Archives Nationales**. This museum houses famous French documents, including some written by Joan of Arc, Marie-Antoinette and Napoléon. It's located in the **Hôtel de Clisson,** a palace dating back to 1371, the highlight of which is the incredibly ornate, oval-shaped **Salon Ovale**. It's closed on Tuesday.

Rue des Francs-Bourgeois becomes rue Rambuteau. As you pass rue du Temple, you'll begin to see your final stop.

You can't miss the **Centre Georges Pompidou** (a fantastic modern-art museum) at place Georges-Pompidou. The building is a work of art in itself. The controversial building is "ekoskeletal" (all the plumbing, elevators and ducts are exposed and brightly painted). There's a great view from the rooftop restaurant (**Georges**). Don't miss the **Stravinsky Fountain** with its moving mobile sculptures and circus atmosphere just to the south of the museum. Notice the red pouty lips in the fountain!

After you've had enough of the museum, head right over to the **Café Beaubourg** facing the museum. It's crowded with an artsy crowd and recommended for a drink and perhaps a snack. The food is not that great, but the bathrooms are worth the trip. Tel. 01/48.87.63.96.

You'll end your walk here and you can take the métro Rambuteau back to your hotel.

MAJOR SIGHTS WALK

Approximate distance: five miles; two miles to place de l'Alma and three miles to Arc de Triomphe. Highlights: Tour Eiffel, Bateaux Mouches, Arc de Triomphe, and Champs-Élysées.

Take the métro to École Militaire.

At the métro stop, you'll see the huge **École Militaire** (it's open only on special occasions). This Royal Military Academy was built in the mid-1700s to educate the sons of military officers. The building is a grand example of the French Classical style with its dome and Corinthian pillars. Its most famous alumnus is Napoléon.

Now start walking toward the Eiffel Tower.

The **Champ-de-Mars** are the long gardens that stretch from the **École Militaire** to the **Tour Eiffel** (Eiffel Tower).

It's time to visit one of the most well-known landmarks in the world. It's best to visit the **Tour Eiffel** in either early morning or

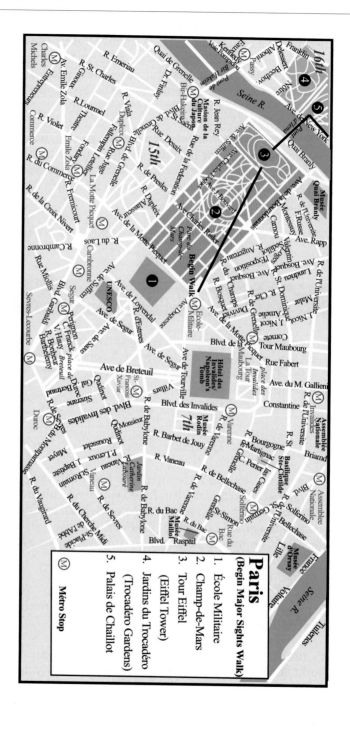

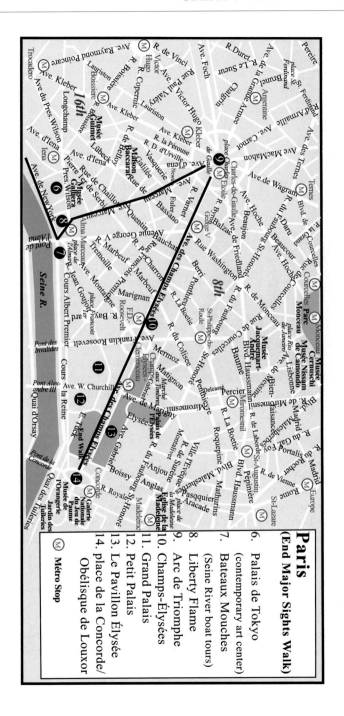

Paris
(End Major Sights Walk)

6. Palais de Tokyo (contemporary art center)
7. Bateaux Mouches (Seine River boat tours)
8. Liberty Flame
9. Arc de Triomphe
10. Champs-Élysées
11. Grand Palais
12. Petit Palais
13. Le Pavillon Élysée
14. place de la Concorde/Obélisque de Louxor

Ⓜ Métro Stop

late evening when the crowds are smaller. Created for the 1889 Universal Exhibition, the Eiffel Tower was built by the same man who designed the framework for the Statue of Liberty. At first it was called, among other things, an "iron monster" when it was erected. Gustave-Alexandre Eiffel never meant for his 7,000-ton tower to be permanent, and it was almost torn down in 1909. Today, it's without doubt the most recognizable structure in the world. Well over 200 million people have visited this monument. You can either take the elevator to one of three landings, or climb the 1,652 stairs.

Walk behind the Eiffel Tower and cross the bridge (the Pont d'Iéna).

Once you cross the bridge, you'll be in the **Jardins du Trocadéro** (Trocadéro Gardens), home to the **Palais de Chaillot**. This huge palace, surrounded by more than 60 fountains, was built 60 years ago, and is home to several museums, including a marine museum. Also here at the foot of the palace is the new **CinéAqua**, a splashy aquarium.

After taking in the gardens and palace, turn right (as you face the palace and gardens) on the avenue de New York along the Seine River.

While you're on the avenue de New York, you'll see the **Palais de Tokyo** on the left, a contemporary art center (and one of the most glamorous places for skateboarders).

Follow avenue de New York until you reach the Pont de l'Alma (the second bridge).

This bridge, the **Pont de l'Alma**, was created in the time of Napoléon III. The original bridge was replaced in 1972 with the present-day steel structure. Take a look at one of the fanciest high-water markers in the world. Originally, there were four Second Empire soldier statues that decorated the old bridge. Only one, Zouave, remains below the bridge. Parisians use it to measure the height of the water in the Seine. It's said that in 1910, the water reached all the way to Zouave's chin.

You're now at the **place de l'Alma**, one of the most luxurious areas in Paris.

If you have never been in Paris (or for that matter, even if you have), you might want to take a tour of the Seine on the **Bateaux Mouches**. These boats depart from the Right Bank next to the place de l'Alma.

At the place de l'Alma, you'll see a replica of the torch of the Statue of Liberty.

The replica of the torch of the Statue of Liberty was erected here in 1987. It was meant to commemorate the French Resistance during World War II. It just happens to be over the tunnel where Princess Diana and her boyfriend Dodi Al-Fayedh were killed in an automobile crash in 1997. The **Liberty Flame** is now an unofficial shrine covered with notes, flowers and prayers to the dead princess.

If you've had enough walking, here's a good place to take the métro Alma Marceau back to your hotel. But if you want to continue, head down the avenue Marceau. It's one of the streets off of place de l'Alma. It's about a 10-minute walk on avenue Marceau to the Arc de Triomphe.

When you get to the **Arc de Triomphe**, don't try to walk across the square. This is Paris's busiest intersection. Twelve avenues pour into the circle around the Arc. There are underground passages, however, that take you to the monument. There's an observation deck providing one of the greatest views of Paris. There's no cost to visit the Arc, but there's an admission fee for the exhibit of photos of the Arc throughout history and for the observation deck. If you aren't impressed by the view down the Champs-Élysées, you really shouldn't have come to Paris.

Tired? If so, here's a good place to take the métro Charles-de-Gaulle-Étoile back to your hotel. But if you want to continue, head down the Champs-Élysées.

The left side of the **Champs-Élysées** has more interesting establishments than the banks and businesses on the right side. This street is one of the most famous in the world. It's home to expensive retail shops, fast-food chains, car dealers, banks, huge movie theatres and overpriced cafés. Despite this, you can sit at a café and experience great people-watching (mostly tourists).

One interesting shop is the large **Sephora Perfume Store** at 74 Champs-Élysées (open daily until midnight). The large "wheel of scents" lets you smell scents from chocolate to flower to wood!

On the left side, toward the end of the Champs-Élysées (at number 10) is **Le Pavillon Élysée**, an elegant oblong glass building built for the 1900 World's Fair. It's home to **Lenôtre**, a café, kitchen shop and cooking school all in one. A shrine to food in the heart of Paris. Lenôtre's specialty is its desserts, and you can enjoy one with a cup of delicious coffee on the lovely stone terrace that looks onto the gardens.

At avenue Winston-Churchill you can gaze at the recently renovated **Grand** and **Petit Palais**, both built for the 1900 World

Exhibition and, like the Eiffel Tower, never meant to be permanent structures. These magnificent buildings remain today in all their glory. The Grand Palais hosts changing art exhibits and the Petit Palais houses the city's fine-arts museum.

Continue down the Champs-Élysées until you reach the huge place de la Concorde.

At the end of your walk, admire the huge **place de la Concorde**. In the center of these 21 acres stands the **Obélisque de Louxor** (Obelisk of Luxor), an Egyptian column from the 13th century covered with hieroglyphics. It was moved here in 1833. Now a traffic roundabout, it was here that Louis XVI and Marie-Antoinette were guillotined during the French Revolution.

You can take the Métro Concorde back to your hotel. The métro stop is at the far left side of the place de la Concorde.

The **Concorde métro** stop has 44,000 blue-and-white lettered ceramic tiles on its walls. Don't read French? I always wondered if they meant anything. In fact, they do. They spell out the seventeen articles of the declaration of the *Rights of Man and the Citizens* that the French National Assembly adopted in 1789.

MONTMARTRE WALK

Approximate distance: two miles. Highlights: Sacré-Coeur, Espace Salvador Dali, and Moulin Rouge. Note: There are lots of steps and steep, cobbled streets on this walk.

Your walk begins at the Abbesses métro stop.

This métro stop is the deepest in Paris and stands on the site of a medieval abbey. You'll know this right away as there are tons of stairs to climb just to get out of the métro. You can also take an elevator to the top.

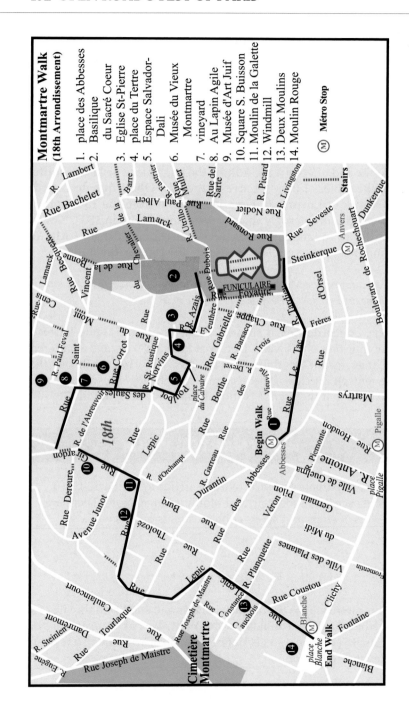

Montmartre Walk
(18th Arrondissement)

1. place des Abbesses
2. Basilique
   du Sacré Coeur
3. Eglise St-Pierre
4. place du Tertre
5. Espace Salvador-
   Dali
6. Musée du Vieux
   Montmartre
   vineyard
7. Au Lapin Agile
8. Musée d'Art Juif
9. Square S. Buisson
10. Moulin de la Galette
11. Windmill
12. Deux Moulins
13. Moulin Rouge
14. Moulin Rouge

Ⓜ Métro Stop

When you get out of the métro, you'll be at the **place des Abbesses**. Take in the picturesque triangular "square" which features one of the few remaining curvy, green wrought-iron Art Nouveau entrances.

Off of the place des Abbesses, take rue Yvonne-Le-Tac which becomes rue Tardieu.

You'll be at the base of the **Basilique du Sacré-Coeur** (Sacred Heart Basilica). It's at the top of the hill (*butte*) and dominates this

neighborhood. You can't miss the Basilica with its white onion domes and Byzantine and Romanesque architecture. Completed in 1919, it's named for Christ's sacred heart which some believe is in the crypt. Inside, you'll find gold mosaics, but the real treat is the view of Paris from the dome.

You have three ways to get to the Basilica. For the price of a métro ticket, you can take the funicular (cable car). You can also take the 224 steps up rue Foyatier (to the left of the cable car) – one of the most photographed sights in Paris – or you can take the steps directly in front of the Basilica.

With the Basilica to your back, turn to the right and follow rue Azaïs and then take a right onto rue St-Eleuthère.

On your right will be the **Eglise St-Pierre**, one of the oldest churches in Paris. The Roman marble columns date back to the 1100s.

Detour

If you need a break after visiting the Basilica, stop at the picturesque **Café L'Été en Pente Douce** (which means "summer on a gentle slope") at 23 rue Muller. If you're facing the Basilica, take the steps down to your right (rue Maurice-Utrillo) and at the bottom is rue Muller and the café.

Head down rue Norvins (it's to your left with the Eglise St-Pierre to your back) through the place du Tertre.

The attractive **place du Tertre** is overrun with tourists and artists trying to paint your portrait. There's a circus-like atmosphere here.

Across the square is the short rue du Calvaire. Turn right into the place du Calvaire (right before you reach the stairs heading down the hill).

On the other side of this attractive square is our next stop, **Espace Salvador-Dali**, at 11 rue Poulbot. Black walls, weird music with Dali's voice and dim lighting all make this museum an interesting experience. Come here if you're a fan of Salvador Dali to see 300 of his lithographs and etchings and 25 sculptures.

Continue on rue Poulbot, make a left on rue Norvins and a quick right down rue des Saules.

Detour

Take a right onto beautiful rue Cortot to visit the **Musée du Vieux Montmartre** at 12 rue Cortot. Renoir and van Gogh are just a couple of the artists who have occupied this 17th-century house. It now has a collection of mementos of the neighborhood, including paintings, posters and photographs.

Continue down rue des Saules.

On your right is the last remaining **vineyard** in Paris at the corner of rue St-Vincent and rue des Saules near the place Jules Joffrin. They still sell wine here. The labels are designed by local artists. The harvesting of the grapes in October gives the residents of Montmartre yet another excuse to have a festival.

You'll likely hear French folk tunes coming out of the shuttered cottage at the picturesque intersection of rue des Saules and rue St-Vincent. **Au Lapin Agile/Cabaret des Assassins** was once frequented by Picasso. Today, you'll sit at small wooden tables and listen to *chansonniers* (singers). A truly Parisian experience.

Turn left on rue St-Vincent and make a left at place Constantine Pecquer. Climb the stairs (yes, more stairs!). At the top is rue Girardon.

The park on your right is **Square Suzanne Buisson**, named after a leader of the French Resistance. According to legend, St-Denis (after being decapitated) carried his head here and washed it in the fountain. There's a statue of him holding his head.

Detour

If you're interested in ancient and modern Jewish art, you can continue down the many stairs of rue des Saules to the Musée d'Art Juif at 42 rue des Saules. It's closed Friday, Saturday and August.

Follow rue Girardon until you reach the corner of rue Lepic.

In the 19th century, Montmartre had many vineyards and over 40 windmills. One of the two surviving windmills, the **Moulin de la Galette**, is on this corner. If it looks familiar, it's the windmill depicted by Renoir in his painting of the same name. It's now part of a restaurant.

From here turn right on rue Lepic.

You'll see the other surviving **windmill** on your right at the corner of rue Tholozé.

Continue downhill (finally!) on rue Lepic.

You may want to have a glass of wine at **O'Vinéa**, a wine bar at 69 rue Lepic.

Van Gogh lived at 54 rue Lepic in 1886.

The movie *Amélie* won not only many film awards, but also a cult following. The lead character is a waitress. You can visit Amélie's 1950s bistro **Bartabac des Deux Moulins** at 15 rue

Lepic, 18th/Métro Blanche, where you'll find mostly locals enjoying good homemade desserts and standard bistro fare.

At the end of rue Lepic at place Blanche, turn right onto boulevard de Clichy.

At 82 boulevard de Clichy, you'll see the **Moulin Rouge**. Originally a red windmill, this dance hall has been around since 1889. It's without a doubt the most famous cabaret in the world. Toulouse-Lautrec memorialized the Moulin Rouge in his paintings, and it got a boost in business from the more recent movie of the same name. Looking for a little bit of Vegas? You'll find it here.

Here, you can head home at the métro Blanche stop (especially if you have kids with you), or you can head left (with the Moulin Rouge to your back) down boulevard de Clichy to place Pigalle.

You come to **place Pigalle** for only one thing: sex. Littered with sex shops, this area was known as "Pig Alley" during World War II.

You can end your trip here at the métro Pigalle stop.

THE DA VINCI CODE WALK

Approximate distance: three miles. Highlights: Hôtel Ritz, Louvre, and Église St-Sulpice.

Much of Dan Brown's wildly popular book *The Da Vinci Code,* takes place in Paris. You'll visit some of the sights featured in the book and movie. Even if you're not a fan of the book, you'll see some of the best sights of Paris on this walk.

Our walk begins at the Opéra métro stop. As you exit the métro, you'll be at the place de l'Opéra.

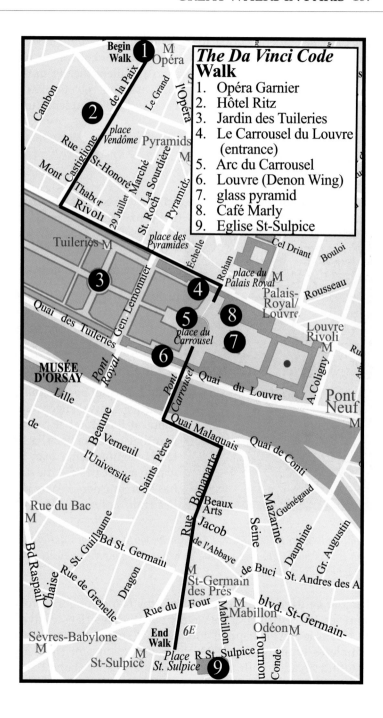

The Da Vinci Code Walk

1. Opéra Garnier
2. Hôtel Ritz
3. Jardin des Tuileries
4. Le Carrousel du Louvre (entrance)
5. Arc du Carrousel
6. Louvre (Denon Wing)
7. glass pyramid
8. Café Marly
9. Eglise St-Sulpice

The place de l'Opéra is home to the **Opéra Garnier**. Built in 1875, this ornate opera house is now the showplace for both opera and dance. It's often referred to as the most opulent theater in the world, with chandeliers, marble stairways, red-velvet boxes, a ceiling painted by Chagall, and a facade of marble and sculpture.

From the place de l'Opéra, head south (in the direction away from the Opéra toward the large column) down rue de la Paix. You'll pass rue des Capucines and arrive at an elegant square.

The **place Vendôme** is the home of a 144-foot column honoring Napoléon. The column is faced with bronze from 1,200 melted

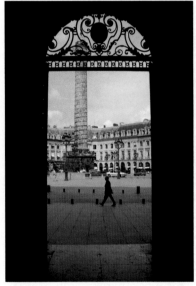

cannons from Austrian and Russian armies. That's Napoléon on top dressed as Julius Caesar. Chopin lived and died at No. 12. Although the Ministry of Justice is here, most notice the luxury hotel on your right at number 15.

Harvard professor Robert Langdon, the book's main character, is awakened in his room at the **Hôtel Ritz**. It's here that inspector Bezu Fache tells Langdon that a man he was to meet earlier in the day has been murdered. Why not head into the luxurious lobby?

From the hotel and the place Vendôme, head south on rue de Castiglione. You'll pass rue St-Honoré and rue du Mont-Thabor before you arrive at rue de Rivoli.

The **rue de Rivoli** was commissioned by Napoléon for victory marches. It's named after his victory over the Austrians at Rivoli in 1797. He never stepped foot on this street, as it was not completed until the mid-1800s, long after his death. There are beautiful arcades with neo-Classical apartments above them.

Today, the arcades house a mixture of souvenir and luxury-goods shops.

Take a left onto rue de Rivoli.

The garden across the street, the **Jardin des Tuileries**, was designed by the same man who planned the gardens of Versailles. The garden takes its name from the word *tuil* or tile (roof-tile factories once were here). This beautiful garden in the middle of Paris is filled with fountains, statues, flowers and trees.

You'll pass rue d'Alger, rue de Juillet 29, rue St-Roch, place des Pyramides (home to a glistening gold equestrian statue of Joan of Arc), and rue de l'Échelle. Cross the street at rue de Rohan.

At 99 rue de Rivoli is the entry to **Le Carrousel du Louvre**, a shopping mall with over 45 stores below the Louvre. Take the escalators down to the lower level of the mall. An inverted glass pyramid drops down into the center of the mall. Look familiar? It was also designed by I.M. Pei, who designed the famous pyramid entry to the Louvre. This is where, according to the book, you'll find the Holy Grail.

There is an entry to the **Musée National du Louvre** here (to your left as you're facing the inverted pyramid).

Simply put, the Louvre is the greatest art museum in the world. It's huge. It's the largest art museum in the world, the largest

building in Paris, and it's in the largest palace in Europe. In the **Denon Wing** you'll find many of Da Vinci's paintings. After the body of Jacques Saunière (the curator at the Louvre) is found here, Robert Langdon and Saunière's granddaughter Sophie Neveu try to unravel the coded message left by Saunière before his death. Two of Da Vinci's paintings featured in the book are found here: the *Mona Lisa* and *Madonna of the Rocks*. You can visit the Louvre now, but I'd save that for another day.

After seeing the inverted pyramid, return to the top of the escalators and take the glass doors to your right. You'll now enter the inner courtyard of the Louvre.

The buildings that house the Louvre were constructed in the 13th century as a fortress. Today, the inner courtyard is the site of the controversial (but I think fantastic) **glass pyramid** designed by the famous architect I.M. Pei, that serves as the main entrance to the museum.

As you're facing the glass pyramid, behind you is the **Arc du Carrousel**, a triumphal arch, topped with four bronze horses, between the Louvre and the Tuileries.

To your left as you're facing the glass pyramid (under the arch that says "Pavillon Turgot") is the **Café Marly**. The setting is

extraordinary, as it overlooks the glass pyramid. *Info*: 1st/Métro Musée du Louvre/Palais-Royal. 93 rue de Rivoli. Tel. 01/ 49.26.06.60. Open daily 8am to 2pm.

You can end your walk here or continue an extra one-and-a-quarter miles to the final destination. You can also navigate the métro from the Palais Royal stop to the St-Sulpice stop if you do not want to walk.

Let's continue our walk from the outdoor glass pyramid. Exit south through the three traffic arches (to your right if you're facing the glass pyramid). You'll cross the Seine River on the bridge, the Pont du Carrousel. Walk on the left side of the bridge.

After you've crossed the bridge, head left and cross the street at the first crosswalk on Quai Malaquais. You'll then make a right onto rue Bonaparte. You'll pass rue Jacob, boulevard St-Germain-des-Prés, and rue du Four before you arrive at our final destination.

Located on an attractive square with a lovely fountain (the **Fontaine-des-Quatre Points**), the **Eglise St-Sulpice** has one of the largest pipe organs in the world with over 6,700 pipes. You'll notice that one of the two bell towers was never completed. Inside are frescoes by Delacroix in the Chapel of the Angels (**Chapelle des Anges**), a statue of the Virgin and child by Pigalle, and Servandoni's Chapel of the Madonna (**Chapelle de la Madone**).

It was here that Silas, an albino monk, brutally kills a nun. He has visited the church in a quest to find a keystone that would unlock the secret of the Holy Grail. Set into the floor of the aisle of the north-south transept is a bronze line marking the Rose Line. On the two equinoxes and the winter solstice, the sun reflects onto a globe and obelisk and from there to a crucifix. The obelisk reads: "Two scientists with God's help."

Fans of the book and movie are also searching the church for a stained-glass window with the intertwined letters P and S, which the book contends stands for the Priory of Sion. Robert Langdon describes the Priory of Sion as a secret society formed in the 11th century dedicated to the preservation of the bloodline of Jesus. Can you locate the stained-glass window?

After visiting the church, take a break at one of the lovely cafés here on the square.

CULINARY WALKS

Approximate distance: a quarter of a mile. **Highlights:** Lavinia (wine shop) and Fauchon (culinary souvenirs). Note that most are closed on Sunday.

This short walk is packed with specialty-food shops, wine dealers, restaurants, and tea rooms.

*Take the métro to the Madeleine stop. Your walk begins at the **place de la Madeleine** in the 8th. Begin at Lavinia and continue around the square.*

•**Lavinia** *(number 3-5)*
The largest wine shop in Paris with wines priced from 3 to 3,600 euros. Drink any bottle from the shop at the wine bar. Lunch served – with wine, of course. No dinner.

•**Boutique Maille** *(number 6)*
Boutique mustard shop.

•**L'Ecluse** *(number 15)*
Chain of trendy wine bars. Not the greatest food in Paris, but great for wine tasting (especially Bordeaux).

•**Caviar Kaspia** *(number 17)*
Caviar, blinis and salmon. There's also a restaurant upstairs.

•**Hédiard** *(number 21)*
Food store/spice shop that's been open since the 1850s, similar to Fauchon, with an on-site restaurant.

•**Nicolas** *(number 31)*
Located upstairs from the Nicolas

wine shop. You can buy a bottle of wine at the shop and have it served with your meal. The menu is limited, but the wines sold by the glass are inexpensive.

•**Fauchon** *(number 26)*
Deli and grocery known for its huge selection of canned food, baked goods and alcohol. The store is a must for those wanting to bring back French specialties.

•**La Maison du Miel** *(located around the corner from Fauchon at 24 rue Vignon)*
This food store contains everything made from honey (from sweets to soap).

•**Marquise de Sévigné** *(number 32)*
A French "luxury" (their word) chocolate maker since 1898.

There are several areas in Paris where many restaurants are concentrated in small pockets:

• **Rue Pot-de-Fer** between la rue Tournefort and la rue Mouffetard, just off the market. (5th/Métro Monge).
• **Passage Brady** (enter around 33 boulevard de Strasbourg) with inexpensive Indian, Turkish, and Moroccan restaurants.(10th/Métro Château d'Eau).
• **Place Ste-Catherine** (enter

Best Markets in Paris

Unless noted otherwise, these markets are open Tuesday through noon on Sunday. Some of the best-known are:

• **Rue Montorgueil** (1st/ Métro Les Halles)
• **Rue Mouffetard** (5th/ Métro Censier-Daubenton)
• **Rue de Buci** (6th/Métro Mabillon)
• **Rue Cler** (7th/Métro École Militaire)
• **Marché Bastille** on the boulevard Richard Lenoir (11th/Métro Bastille) (open Thursday and Sunday)
• **Rue Daguerre** (14th/ Métro Denfert-Rochereau)
• **Rue Poncelet** (17th/Métro Ternes)

from rue Caron off of rue St-Antoine) in the Marais. Overlooking the square is **Soprano**, serving delicious authentic Italian dishes. Tel. 01/42.72.37.21. (4th/Métro St-Paul).

• **Off of la rue St-Jacques** in the area around la rue St-Séverin and la rue de la Huchette for French, Italian, Greek and other restaurants jammed into small streets. (5th/Métro St-Michel).

7. BEST SLEEPS & EATS

I've presented only the very best in each price category so you won't waste your time figuring out where to stay and eat.

A hotel room in Paris is nowhere near the size of a hotel room in the U.S. and Canada. Rooms generally are quite small. When you're in Paris, you should be out seeing the great city anyway, so you probably won't spend that much time in your room. If size is an issue, why not try renting an apartment? Tips on renting an apartment are listed later in this chapter.

Food in Paris is, for the most part, superb. I suspect this is one of the main reasons you've come here! You will find fantastic cuisine and great wine if you follow the suggestions in this chapter.

Note that lunch is served from noon to around 2pm, and dinner from 8pm to 11pm. Restaurants usually have two seatings: at 8 or 8:30pm, and at 10 or 10:30pm. The restaurant will be less crowded at the early seating. **Make reservations!**

BEST SLEEPS

It can be difficult to find a hotel during the large trade fairs in January, March, May, early July, September and October, so plan ahead. During these times, plenty of apartments are available for rent.

Note: Prices given are for double rooms.

EXPENSIVE (over €200)
Castille
Lovely hotel (with 86 rooms and 21 suites) in a 19th-century building with French and Venetian-style interior near the place

Vendôme with a very helpful staff and subtle décor. The hotel is undergoing a renovation of all floors and those that have been completed are especially nice. Suites are lovely. This Italian-owned hotel is home to the excellent Il Cortile Italian restaurant. Perfect for those looking to shop at the nearby upscale boutiques (it's next door to the Chanel store). Also a good choice for business travelers as there is a free business center, in-room wireless Internet and voice mail. *Info*: 1st/Métro Concorde or Madeleine. 33/37 rue Cambon. Tel. 01/44.58.44.58 (800/323-7500). www.starhotels.com. €390 (€790 for suites). V, MC, DC, AE. Restaurant, bar, room service, TV, telephone, gym, sauna, concierge, AC, wireless Internet access, minibar, CD player, safe, parking.

George V (Four Seasons)
Luxurious. Considered "the" place to stay in Paris for those with unlimited budgets, you'll find every amenity at this recently renovated hotel. *Info*: 8th/Métro George V.

Credit Card Shorthand

V: Visa
MC: Mastercard
DC: Diners Club
AE: American Express

31 avenue George V. Tel. 01/49.52.70.00 (800/332-3442). www.fourseasons.com/paris/. €710. V, MC, DC, AE. Restaurant, bars, room service, TV, telephone, gym, pool, sauna/steam rooms, whirlpool, spa services, concierge, AC, Internet access, minibar, CD player, safe, parking.

Hôtel Le Colbert

This Left Bank hotel has 39 rooms in a former 19th-century Mansion House. It's located only a block away from the Seine River and some rooms have views of Notre-Dame. It's known for its friendly English-speaking staff and for its excellent location near many fine restaurants. Rooms and bathrooms are small for the most part, but regular visitors to Paris love this place. *Info*: 5th/ Métro St-Michel. 7 rue Hôtel Le Colbert. Tel. 01/56.81.19.00. www.lecolbert.com. €335. V, MC, AE. Bar, satellite TV, telephone, concierge, AC, Internet access, minibar, safe.

Hôtel Les Jardins du Trocadéro

This hotel overlooks the place du Trocadéro, just a short walk to the Eiffel Tower and upscale shopping. Stone walls, stylish furniture in this 18th-century building with all the modern conveniences. 16th/Métro Trocadéro. 35 rue Benjamin-Franklin. Tel. 01/53.70.17.70. www.academiehotel.com. €299. V, MC, DC, AE. Restaurant, bar, room service, satellite TV, telephone, concierge, AC, Internet access, minibar, safe.

Jeu de Paume

Located on one of the most beautiful streets in all of Paris, this hotel has an excellent location on the Île St-Louis. Lovely courtyard and tastefully decorated. *Info*: 4th/Métro Pont Marie. 54 rue St-Louis-en-l'Île. Tel. 01/43.26.14.18. www.jeudepaumehotel.com. €205-335/V, MC, DC AE. 30 rooms, 2 apartments, dining room, game room, music room, library, billiard room, bar, room service until 11pm, TV, telephone, gym, sauna, concierge, no AC, wireless Internet access, safe, disabled access, pets welcome.

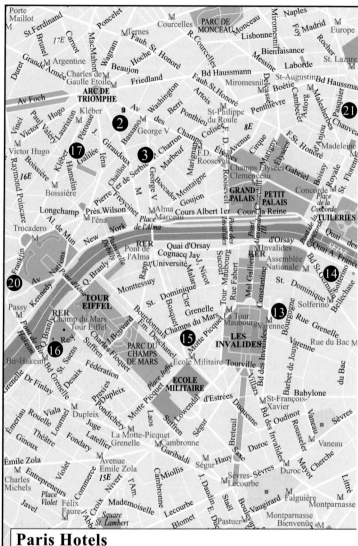

Paris Hotels

1. Castille
2. Galileo
3. George V
4. Grand Hôtel Jeanne d'Arc
5. Grand Hôtel Malher
6. Hospitel Hôtel Dieu
7. Hôtel Axial Beaubourg
8. Hôtel Beaubourg
9. Hôtel Britannique
10. Hôtel Collège de France
11. Hôtel de l'Académie
12. Hôtel des Deux-Îles
13. Hôtel de Varenne
14. Hôtel d'Orsay

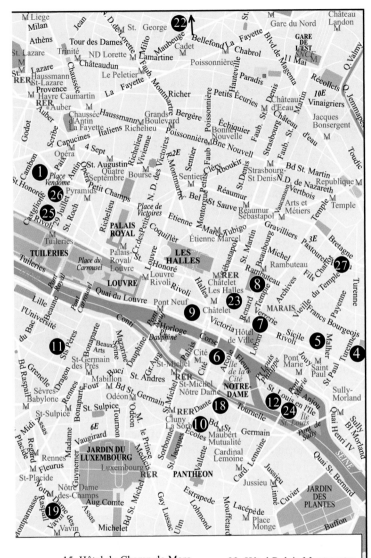

15. Hôtel du Champ de Mars
16. Hôtel Eiffel Seine
17. Hôtel Kléber
18. Hôtel Le Colbert
19. Hôtel Le Sainte-Beuve
20. Hôtel Les Jardins du Trocadéro
21. Hôtel Madeleine Opéra

22. Hôtel Relais Montmartre
23. Hôtel St-Merry
24. Jeu de Paume
25. L'Hôtel Brighton
26. Ritz
27. Saintonge
M Métro Stop

Ritz

Glamorous, very expensive and a favorite of royalty, movie stars

 and presidents-and you'll feel like one among the antiques and luxurious accommodations. *Info*: 1ˢᵗ/ Métro Opéra. 15 place Vendôme. Tel. 01/43.16.30.30 (800/223-6800). www.ritzparis.com. €515. V, MC, DC, AE. Each room has a computer/printer. 2 restaurants, 4 bars, room service, TV, telephone, gym, pool, concierge, AC, wireless Internet access, minibar, safe, Sunday brunch, 7 banquet rooms, massage, beauty salon, parking.

MODERATE (€125-€200)

Galileo

This 27-room hotel is located down a quiet side street near the Arc de Triomphe and the Champs-Élysées. Clean, comfortable and with a helpful staff. *Info*: 8ᵗʰ/Métro George V. 54 rue Galilée. Tel. 01/47.20.66.06. www.galileo-paris-hotel.com. €165. V, MC, DC, AE. TV, telephone, AC, Internet access, minibar, disabled access.

Grand Hôtel Malher

This family-run, friendly and helpful hotel is near the place des Vosges in the heart of the Marais. Small rooms, modern bathrooms and a lovely 18ᵗʰ-century vaulted breakfast room in the cellar. The best of its 31 rooms are numbers 1 and 2, off of the small courtyard. Note that there is no air conditioning. *Info*: 4ᵗʰ/Métro St-Paul or Bastille. 5 rue Malher. Tel. 01/42.72.60.92. www.grandhotelmalher.com. €107-135/€8 breakfast. V, MC. Satellite TV, telephone, minibar.

Hôtel Axial Beaubourg

Despite small rooms, this stylish hotel near the Hôtel de Ville and the Pompidou Center has a devoted following. Contemporary hotel with 58 rooms and suites and modern conveniences. Good shopping nearby. *Info*: 4ᵗʰ/Hôtel de Ville.

Ultra-Lux Hotel Tip

You'll find seven ultra-luxury hotels located in palaces in Paris: Bristol, Crillon, George-V, Meurice, Plaza Athénée, Ritz and Fouquet's Barrière.

11 rue du Temple. Tel. 01/42.72.72.22. www.axialbeaubourg.com. €170 (low season)-200 (high season)/€12-14 breakfast. V, MC, DC, AE. Bar, gym, sauna, satellite TV, telephone, AC, high-speed internet access, safe.

Hôtel Beaubourg

This small 28-room, comfortable hotel is located on a quiet street just steps from the Pompidou Center and within walking distance of most major sights. Its rooms are nicely decorated and its staff is helpful. Breakfast served in a vaulted cellar. *Info*: 4th/Métro  Rambuteau. 11 rue Simon LeFranc. Tel 01/42.74.34.24. www.hotelbeaubourg.com. €115-140. V, MC, DC, AE. Satellite TV, telephone, AC, Internet access available.

Hôtel Britannique

Quiet, friendly, clean and very French hotel on the place du Châtelet. Perfect location near the sights on the islands in the Seine River and the Louvre. *Info*: 1st/Métro Châtelet. 20 ave. Victoria. Tel. 01/42.33.74.59. www.hotel-britannique.fr. €168/€14 breakfast. V, MC, AE. Flat screen TV, AC, Internet access, minibar.

Hôtel de l'Académie

Located in the heart of the St-Germain-des-Prés district, this former mansion, complete with wooden beams and stone walls, has been tastefully restored. Great for shopping at designer boutiques or at antique shops and near the famous duo of cafés: Café de Flore and Les Deux Magots. *Info*: 7th/Métro St-Germain-des-Prés. 32 rue des Sts-Pères. Tel. 01/45.49.80.00. www.academiehotel.com. €200. V, MC, DC, AE. Bar, TV, telephone, concierge, Internet access, parking (€23 per day).

Hôtel des Deux-Îles

This hotel on the Île St-Louis has 17 rooms in a 17th-century townhouse located on one of the most beautiful streets in all of Paris. Fantastic central location. Friendly staff. Space is tight on the islands in the middle of the Seine River and rooms are small. *Info*: 4th/Métro Pont Marie. 59 rue St-Louis-en-l'Île. Tel. 01/43.26.13.35. www.deuxiles-paris-hotel.com. €150-170/€11 break

Hôtel de Varenne

This hotel is in the shadows of Les Invalides and is within blocks of Napoleon's Tomb and the Rodin Museum. It's also about halfway between the Eiffel Tower and the Musée d'Orsay. If the perfect location isn't good enough, the hotel, located in a former private mansion, gets rave reviews for friendliness, cleanliness and charm. The hotel was renovated in 2003. Breakfast is served in the attractive small garden in summer. *Info*: 7th/Métro Varenne. 44 rue de Bourgogne. Tel 01/45.51.45.55. www.varenne-hotel-paris.com. €110-€160/€10 breakfast. V, MC, AE. Limited room service, satellite TV, telephone, AC, wireless Internet access available, minibar, safe.

Hôtel d'Orsay

Housed in two 18th-century buildings near the Musée d'Orsay, this hotel has decent-sized rooms, a pleasant staff and is a good bargain. *Info*: 7th/Métro Solférino. 93 rue de Lille. Tel. 01/47.05.85.54. www.esprit-de-france.com. €130-170/€10 breakfast. V, MC. TV, minibar.

Hôtel Eiffel Seine

This contemporary hotel opened in 2006. Its location, within  walking distance of the Eiffel Tower and across the street from the Bir-Hakeim métro stop, is excellent. Each of the 45 small rooms are decorated in an Art Nouveau style with tiled bathrooms. Some rooms overlook the Seine. There's free parking and many modern amenities that come with a new hotel. *Info*: 15th/Métro Bir-Hakeim. 2 blvd. de Grenelle. Tel. 01/45.78.14.81. www.hotel-eiffel-seine-paris.federal-hotel.com. €110-160/€15 breakfast. V, MC, AE. Limited room service, cable TV, telephone, AC, wireless or broadband Internet access, safe.

Hôtel Kléber

Charming and elegant hotel located between the Arc de Triomphe and the Eiffel Tower. Beautifully decorated with period furniture, paintings and woodwork. The more expensive "executive rooms" have Jacuzzis. *Info*: 16th/Métro Kléber, Boissière or Charles-de-Gaulle-Étoile. 7 rue de Belloy. Tel. 01/47.23.80.22. www.academiehotel.com. €189. V, MC, DC, AE. Restaurant, bar, buffet breakfast, room service, TV, telephone, concierge, AC, wireless Internet access, safe, parking.

Hôtel Le Sainte-Beuve

This small hotel, located on a small street between the Luxembourg Gardens and Tour Montparnasse, has period furniture, an attractive lobby and helpful staff. The location is a bit south, but métro stops are nearby. Cute little bar. It's located on the same street  as the highly recommended restaurant Le Timbre. *Info*: 6th/Métro Vavin or Notre-Dame-des-Champs. 9 rue Ste-Beuve. Tel 01/45.48.20.07. www.hotel-sainte-beuve.fr. €135-280. Bar, cable TV, telephone, AC, Internet access, minibar, safe.

Hôtel Relais Montmartre

This new and comfortable hotel has 26 rooms decorated in different color schemes and with period furniture and old beams. It's located on a quiet street, but near the bustle of the Moulin Rouge and close to Sacré Coeur. If you're looking for a comfortable hotel in Montmartre, this is it. (The hotel is not near the center of Paris and most tourist sights.) *Info*: 18th/Métro Blanche. 6 rue Constance (near rue Lepic). Tel: 01/70 64 25 25. www.relaismontmartre.fr. €150-190/€12 breakfast. V, MC, AE, DC. TV, telephone, concierge, AC, free broadband Internet access, minibar, safe, parking. See Montmartre Map.

Hôtel St-Merry

This unique hotel is located in the old presbytery of the Eglise St-Merri. Stone walls, wooden beams and even one room (#9) has a buttress from the church. Good location near the Pompidou Center. Lots of character, but few amenities. There is no elevator or air conditioning. The attached church dates from the mid-16th century and has a flamboyant Gothic exterior (including lots of gargoyles). Its interior isn't bad, either. The composer Saint-Saëns was once an organist here. The church bell is said to be the oldest in Paris. *Info*: 4th/Métro Hôtel de Ville. 78 rue de la Verrerie. Tel. 01/42.78.14.15. www.hotelmarais.com. €130-€250/V, MC, DC, AE. TV (in suite only), limited room service, safe.

L'Hôtel Brighton

There are 65 rooms in this hotel with a perfect location overlooking the Tuileries Garden and near the Louvre and Musée de l'Orangerie. An elegant entry off the rue de Rivoli, and guest rooms are spacious with high ceilings. *Info*: 1st/Métro Tuileries. 218 rue de Rivoli. Tel. 01/47.03.61.61. www.esprit-de-france.com. €137 to 255/€8 (continental breakfast) or €15 (buffet). V, MC, AE, DC. TV, telephone, AC, safe.

What Floor is This?

What we call the first floor is the *rez-de-chaussée* ("RC" or "0"), the ground floor. The first floor in Paris (*premier étage*) is what we would call the second floor.

INEXPENSIVE (under €125)
Grand Hôtel Jeanne d'Arc
Excellent location in the heart of the Marais near the place des Vosges and the lovely place Ste-Catherine. Clean and comfortable. *Info*: 4th/Métro St-Paul. 3 rue Jarente. Tel. 01/48.87.62.11. www.hoteljeannedarc.com. €82-146/€6 breakfast. V, MC. Satellite TV, room service (mornings only), concierge, Internet access, disabled access.

Hospitel Hôtel Dieu

Smack dab in the middle of the Île de la Cité is this interesting choice for a budget hotel. There are only 14 rooms, and some are used by families visiting the sick in the hospital in which this hotel is located. Great for sightseeing (right on the same square as Notre-Dame). Rooms are contemporary and basic with large bathrooms. Note that there is no air conditioning. *Info*: 4th/Métro Cité. 1 Place du Parvis-Notre-Dame. Tel. 01/44.32.01.00. www.hotel-hospitel.com. €104/€8 breakfast. V, MC. Bar, limited room service, TV, telephone, AC, Internet access, safe, disabled access.

Hôtel Collège de France

This small, family-run hotel has a good Latin Quarter location just south of boulevard St-Germain-des-Prés and near the Musée Cluny. The English-speaking staff adds value to this 29-room budget choice. Room #62 costs a little more, but provides a view and more space. Info: 5th/Métro Cluny-La Sorbonne or Maubert-Mutualité. 7 rue Thénard. Tel. 01/43.26.78.36. www.hotel-collegedefrance.com. €99 (room #62 is €120) /€8 breakfast. V, MC, DC, AE. Cable TV, telephone, no AC, wireless Internet access available, in-room safe.

Hôtel du Champ-de-Mars

Excellent location near the Eiffel Tower and the rue Cler market. This 25-room hotel has small, clean rooms. *Info*: 7th/Métro École Militaire. 7 rue du Champ-de-Mars. Tel. 01/45.51.52.30. www.hotel-du-champ-de-mars.com. €78-105/€7 breakfast. V, MC. TV, telephone, no AC.

Hôtel Madeleine Opéra

Just north of the place de la Madeleine, this 25-room bargain hotel has an excellent location (especially for those interested in shopping at the nearby major department stores). Basic rooms (some with small refrigerators) and bathrooms. The entrance resembles a shop at the beginning of the 20th century. Breakfast is served in your room. *Info*: 8th/Métro Madeleine or Havre-Caumartin. 12 rue Greffulhe. Tel 01/47.42.26.26. www.hotel-madeleine-opera.com. €80-98/€7 breakfast. V, AE. TV, telephone, minibar (soft drinks), safe.

Saintonge

Owned by the same group as the Hôtel St-Merri, this cozy 23-room hotel is located on a peaceful street in the Marais. *Info*: 3rd/Métro République. 16 rue de Saintonge. Tel. 01/42.77.91.13. www.hotelmarais.com. €115-170. V, MC, AE, DC. TV, telephone, minibar.

APARTMENTS

One great way to truly experience life in a European city is to **rent an apartment**. They're usually less expensive and larger than a hotel room. If I didn't have to check out hotels, I would always stay in an apartment. Many come with a washer/dryer combination that allows you to pack less. There are many apartments for rent on the Internet. Here are a few that receive good reviews:

- www.rentalo.com
- www.parisleftbankrental .com
- www.ahparis.com
- www.parisperfect.com
- www.willetvillage.com
- www.justfrance.com
- www.franceforrent.com
- www.parisluxuryrentals.com
- www.provencewest.com
- www.parisbandb.com (apartments and bed and breakfast)

BEST EATS

Prices are for a main course and without wine. My price key is as follows:

- **Inexpensive**: under €10
- **Moderate**: €11 - €20
- **Expensive**: over €21

Lunch, even at the most expensive restaurants listed below, always has a lower fixed price. Credit cards accepted unless noted.

A Few Pointers

The bill in a restaurant is called *l'addition* ... but the bill in a bar is called *le compte* or *la note*; confusing? It's easier if you just make a scribbling motion with your fingers on the palm of your hand.

A **service charge** is almost always added to your bill. Depending on the service, it's sometimes appropriate to leave an additional 5 to 10%. The menu will usually note that service is included (*service compris*). Sometimes this is abbreviated with the letters s.c. The letters s.n.c. stand for *service non compris*; this means that the service is not included in the price, and you must leave a tip. You'll sometimes find *couvert* or cover charge on your menu (a small charge just for placing your butt at the table).

A menu is a fixed-price meal, not that piece of paper listing the food items. If you want what we consider a menu, you need to ask for *la carte*. *La carte* is almost always posted on the front of the restaurant so you know what you're getting into, both foodwise and pricewise, before you enter.

Menu Translator Guide!

To help you decipher menus written in French, get *Eating & Drinking in Paris*. It has a comprehensive menu translator, restaurant reviews, and is co-authored by me!

Tips on Budget Dining
There's no need to spend a lot of money in Paris to have good food. Of course it hurts when the dollar is weaker than the euro, but there are all kinds of fabulous foods to be had inexpensively all over Paris.

Eat at a neighborhood restaurant or bistro. The menu, with prices, is posted in the window. Never order anything whose price is not known in advance. If you see *selon grosseur* (sometimes abbreviated as s/g), this means that you're paying by weight, which can be extremely expensive. Avoid restaurants and bistros with English menus.

Delis and food stores can provide cheap and wonderful meals. Buy some cheese, bread, wine and other snacks and have a picnic. in one of Paris's great parks.

Lunch, even at the most expensive restaurants listed in this guide, always has a lower fixed price. So, have lunch as your main meal.

Large department stores frequently have supermarkets (in the basement) and restaurants that have reasonably priced food. And street vendors generally sell inexpensive, terrific food.

For the cost of a cup of coffee or a drink, you can linger at a café and watch the world pass you by for as long as you want.

Phone numbers, days closed and hours of operation often change, so it's advisable to check ahead. Restaurants in tourist areas may have different hours and days of operation during low season. Reservations are recommended for all restaurants unless noted. The telephone country code for France is 33. When calling within France you must dial the area code. The area code for Paris is 01. However, you do not use the 0 before the area code when calling France from the U.S. or Canada.

Left Bank

EXPENSIVE
L'Atelier de Joël Robuchon
Famous chef Joël Robuchon's restaurant where "foodies" sit at the counter sampling innovative dishes. *Info*: 7th/Métro Rue du Bac. 5 rue de Montalembert. Tel. 01/42.22.56.56. Open daily. Reservations accepted for 6:30pm seating only. Expensive.

Gaya
Chef Pierre Gagnaire has taken a fish house and converted it into a sleek restaurant serving superb (and very expensive) seafood. *Info*: 7th/Métro Rue du Bac. 44 rue du Bac. Tel. 01/45.44.73.73. www.pierregagnaire.com. Closed Sun. Expensive.

Vin Sur Vin
Great wine and creative cuisine near the Eiffel Tower. *Info*: 7th/Métro Alma Marceau. 20 rue de Monttessuy. Tel. 01/47.05.14.20. Closed Sat (lunch), Sun & Mon (lunch). Moderate-Expensive.

MODERATE
Allard
Diners repeatedly praise the food at this typical Parisian bistro. The signature dish is *canard aux olives* (duck roasted with olives).

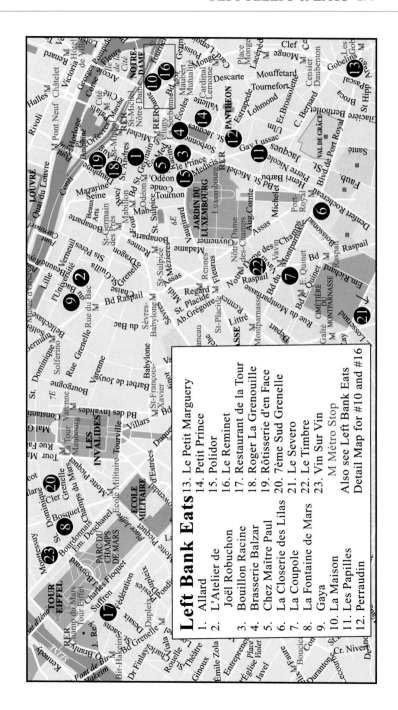

Left Bank Eats
1. Allard
2. L'Atelier de
   Joël Robuchon
3. Bouillon Racine
4. Brasserie Balzar
5. Chez Maître Paul
6. La Closerie des Lilas
7. La Coupole
8. La Fontaine de Mars
9. Gaya
10. La Maison
11. Les Papilles
12. Perraudin
13. Le Petit Marguery
14. Petit Prince
15. Polidor
16. Le Reminet
17. Restaurant de la Tour
18. Roger La Grenouille
19. Rôtisserie d'en Face
20. 7ème Sud Grenelle
21. Le Severo
22. Le Timbre
23. Vin Sur Vin

M Métro Stop

Also see Left Bank Eats
Detail Map for #10 and #16

Info: 6th/Métro Odéon. 41 rue St-André-des-Arts. Tel. 01/ 43.26.48.23. Closed Sun & part of Aug. Moderate.

Bouillon Racine
Popular brasserie serving Belgian cuisine in a historic building. Try the *waterzooi* (chicken or fish poached in a sauce with vegetables). They also often offer a large vegetarian plate. The bar has a huge beer selection. *Info*: 6th/Métro Cluny-La Sorbonne or Odéon. 3 rue Racine. Tel. 01/44.32.15.60. www.bouillon-racine.com. Moderate.

Brasserie Balzar
This Latin Quarter brasserie opened in 1898 and serves traditional French cuisine. It's known for its *poulet rôti* (roast chicken), onion soup and "colorful" waiters. Open daily until midnight. *Info*: 5th/Métro Cluny-La Sorbonne. 49 rue des Écoles. Tel. 01/43.54.13.67. www.brasseriebalzar.com. Moderate.

Chez Maître Paul
Hearty cooking of the Jura Mountains and Franche-Comté regions of France (near the Swiss border), which are known for their game and trout dishes. *Info*: 6th/Métro Odéon. 12 rue Monsieur-le-Prince. Tel. 01/43.54.74.59. Closed part of Aug. Moderate.

La Closerie des Lilas
Lenin and Trotsky are among those who have visited this historic café. There's a terrace, piano bar, *brasserie* (moderate) and restaurant (expensive). The *brasserie* is known for its steak tartare (raw chopped beef). *Info*: 14th/Métro Raspail or Vavin. 171 boulevard du Montparnasse. Tel. 01/40.51.34.50. Moderate-Expensive.

La Coupole
A Montparnasse institution since the days of Picasso, this noisy *brasserie* is a favorite among tourists. It's known for its oysters. Open daily until 1 a.m. *Info*: 14th/Métro Vavin. 102 boulevard du Montparnasse. Tel. 01/43.20.14.20. www.lacoupoleparis.com. Moderate.

La Fontaine de Mars

Red-checked tablecloths, friendly service and reasonable prices near the Eiffel Tower. Try the *poulet fermier aux morilles* (free-range chicken with morel mushrooms). *Info*: 7th/Métro École-Militaire. 129 rue St-Dominique. Tel. 01/47.05.46.44. Next door is **L'Auvergne Gourmande**. Group dining where everyone sits on high stools in a small, fun room (Tel. 01/47.05.60.79). Moderate.

La Maison

An interesting crowd is found at this Latin Quarter bistro located near the Seine. In good weather, the tables on the small square in front of the restaurant are a great place to dine. Try the *épaule d'agneau de sept heures* (shoulder of lamb cooked for seven hours). *Info*: 5th/Métro St-Michel. 1 rue de la Bûcherie. Tel. 01/43.29.73.57. Closed Mon. Moderate.

Les Papilles

Near the Panthéon, Les Papilles (Tastebuds) sells gourmet foods and wine, and offers creative takes on classic French cuisine. Definitely worth the trip! *Info*: 5th/Métro Cluny-La Sorbonne (or RER Luxembourg). 30 rue Gay-Lussac. Tel. 01/43.25.20.79. Closed Sun. Moderate.

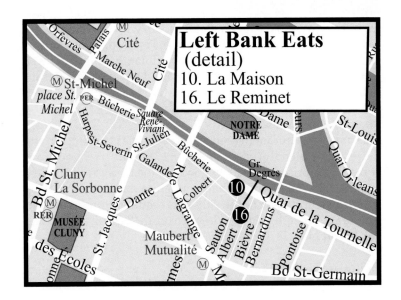

Left Bank Eats (detail)
10. La Maison
16. Le Reminet

Le Petit Marguery
This 1930s bistro features game dishes and is known for its Grand Marnier *soufflé* and its good service. *Info*: 13th/Métro Gobelins. 9 boulevard de Port-Royal. Tel. 01/43.31.58.59. Closed Sun, Mon & Aug. Moderate.

Petit Prince
Walk through the velvet curtains and enter the intimate dining room at this friendly restaurant with an interesting crowd. Try the duck with pear sauce and the chocolate desserts. *Info*: 5th/ Métro Maubert-Mutualité. 12 rue de Lanneau. Tel. 01/43.54.77.26. Open daily. Moderate.

Le Reminet
Small Latin Quarter bistro with modern French cooking and attentive service. Try the grilled lamb when available. Outdoor  seating in the summer. *Info*: 5th/ Métro Maubert-Mutualité. 5 rue des Grands-Degrés. Tel. 01/ 44.07.04.24. Closed Tue, Wed & part of Aug. Moderate.

Restaurant de la Tour
You'll be welcomed by the friendly owners to the lovely dining room with Provençal décor where you'll dine on classic French fare. Try the delicious *sanglier* (wild boar). After dinner, head to the brilliantly lit Eiffel Tower, just a few blocks away. *Info*: 15th/Métro Dupleix. 6 rue Desaix. Tel. 01/43.06.04.24. Closed Sun and Mon. Moderate.

Roger La Grenouille
This quirky restaurant (it seems that everyone is having fun and the service is friendly) was founded in 1930 and serves good food at moderate prices. Especially good are the *coq au vin* and the *tournedos Rossini*. If you've had enough to drink, you may find yourself wearing one of the silly hats scattered throughout the restaurant. *Info*: 6th/Métro Odéon. 26 rue des Grands-Augustins. Tel. 01/56.24.24.34. Closed Sun. Moderate.

La Rôtisserie d'en Face
Modern *rôtisserie* in the St-Germain area known for its imagina-

tive dishes. Lots of grilled dishes on the menu. *Info*: 6th/Métro Odéon or St-Michel. 2 rue Christine. Tel. 01/43.26.40.98. www.jacques-cagna.com. Closed Sat (lunch) and Sun. Moderate.

7ème Sud Grenelle
The odd name means that this restaurant is in the 7th arrondissement at the south end of rue Grenelle. This small modern restaurant serves French, Mediterranean (lots of pasta dishes) and North African (try the *tangine*) cuisine. Friendly service. *Info*: 7th/Métro La Tour-Maubourg. 159 rue de Grenelle. Tel. 01/44.18.30.30. Moderate.

Le Severo
Small bistro away from the tourists. The chef used to be a butcher and the beef here is fantastic. I'd make the trip just for the fries! The wine blackboard fills a whole wall of this bistro. Looking for a truly Parisian experience? This is the place. *Info*: 14th/Métro Alesia. 8 rue des Plantes. Tel. 01/45.40.40.91. Closed Sat (dinner) and Sun. Moderate.

INEXPENSIVE
Perraudin
You'll get to know your fellow diners at this inexpensive bistro steps from the Panthéon serving traditional Parisian cuisine. *Info*: 5th/Métro Cluny-La Sorbonne. 157 rue Saint-Jacques. Tel. 01/46.33.15.75. No reservations. No credit cards. Closed Sat, Sun & part of Aug. Inexpensive-Moderate.

Polidor
Popular 1930s bistro serving traditional Parisian cuisine. *Info*: 6th/Métro Odéon. 41 rue Monsieur-le-Prince. Tel. 01/43.26.95.34. No reservations. No credit cards. Inexpensive.

Le Timbre
The name means "stamp" which is appropriate for this tiny Left Bank bistro. A wonderful Parisian experience. How does the

English chef turn out such wonderful dishes in such a small kitchen? *Info*: 6th/Métro Notre-Dame-des-Champs. 3 rue Ste-Beuve (off of rue Notre-Dame-des-Champs). Closed Sun & part of Aug. Tel. 01/45.49.10.40. Inexpensive-Moderate.

Right Bank

Right Bank
EXPENSIVE
La Cave Gourmande
Raves for chef Mark Singer's cuisine, but not for the trip out to this "remote" part of Paris. "Foodies" love this place, and we had one of our best meals here. *Info*: 19th/Métro Danube or Botzaris. 10 rue du Général-Brunet. Tel. 01/40.40.03.30. Closed Sat, Sun & part of Aug. Moderate-Expensive.

Le Train Bleu
Forget all the food you've eaten in train stations. It's delicious here. But you don't really come here for the food anyway because the setting, with its murals of the French-speaking world, is spectacular. A great place to have a drink. Open daily until 11 p.m. *Info*: 12th/Métro Gare de Lyon. In the Gare de Lyon train station. 20 boulevard Diderot (See Right Bank Eats East Map). Tel. 01/43.43.09.06. www.le-train-bleu.com. Expensive.

Gaspard de la Nuit
This cozy restaurant is located in the Marais between the place de la Bastille and place des Vosges. Traditional French cuisine. Try the delicious *carré d'agneau en croûte d'herbes* (loin of lamb with herbs). *Info*: 4th/Métro Bastille. 6 rue des Tournelles (See Right Bank Eats East Map). Tel. 01/42.77.90.53. www.legaspard.com. Moderate-Expensive.

Il Cortile
Located in the Castille Hotel near the place Vendôme, this excellent restaurant with very attentive service features Italian food. In fine weather, dine on the lovely outdoor terrace. Extensive Italian

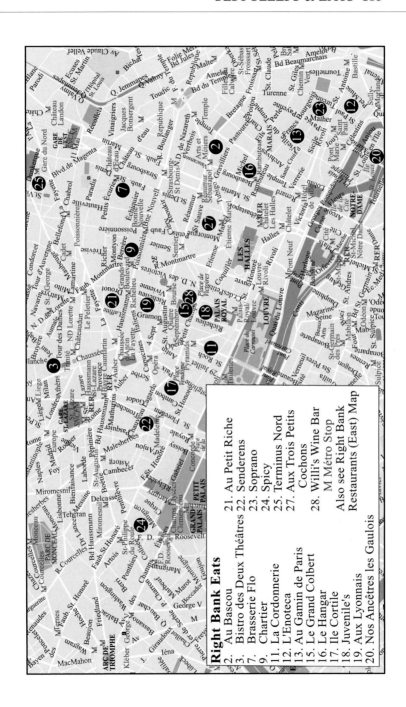

Right Bank Eats
2. Au Bascou
3. Bistro des Deux Théâtres
7. Brasserie Flo
9. Chartier
11. La Cordonnerie
12. L'Enoteca
13. Au Gamin de Paris
15. Le Grand Colbert
16. Le Hangar
17. Ile Cortile
18. Juvenile's
19. Aux Lyonnais
20. Nos Ancêtres les Gaulois
21. Au Petit Riche
22. Senderens
23. Soprano
24. Spicy
25. Terminus Nord
27. Aux Trois Petits
    Cochons
28. Willi's Wine Bar
M Métro Stop
    Also see Right Bank
    Restaurants (East) Map

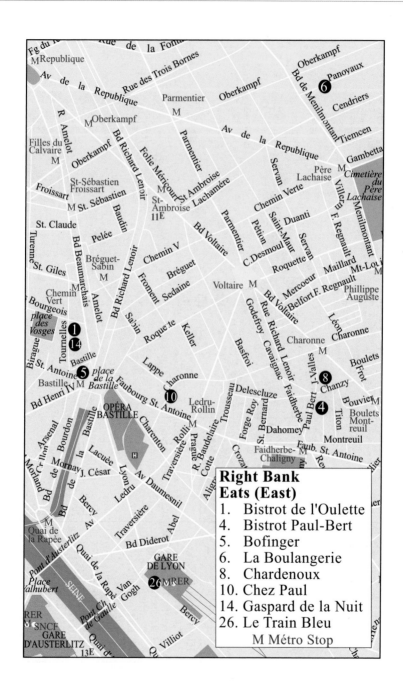

Right Bank Eats (East)
1. Bistrot de l'Oulette
4. Bistrot Paul-Bert
5. Bofinger
6. La Boulangerie
8. Chardenoux
10. Chez Paul
14. Gaspard de la Nuit
26. Le Train Bleu
M Métro Stop

wine list. Try the *pappardelle* with rabbit. *Info*: 1st/Métro Concorde or Madeleine. 33/37 rue Cambon. Tel. 01/44/58/44/58. Expensive.

Senderens
Chef Alain Senderens, a pioneer of *nouvelle cuisine*, ran the restaurant Lucas Carton. He's
changed the name, given Michelin back its stars and (gasp!) lowered prices, although it's still quite expensive. Always elegant, always innovative and always delicious. *Info*: 8th/Métro Madeleine. 9 place de la Madeleine. Tel. 01/42.65.22.90. Closed weekends in July and Aug. Expensive.

Spicy
This restaurant has an excellent location near the Champs-Élysées. Modern French cuisine is served by a friendly, English-speaking staff to an international clientele. The roasted chicken is a good choice. Excellent desserts (try the chocolate cake). The house red Bordeaux is an excellent value at less than €20 per bottle. The only thing "wrong" with this restaurant is its name, as the food served here isn't particularly spicy. *Info*: 8th/Métro F.D.-Roosevelt. 8 ave. F.D.-Roosevelt. Tel. 01/56.59.62.59. Open daily for lunch and dinner. www.spicyrestaurant.com. Moderate-Expensive.

MODERATE
Au Bascou
Modern bistro near the place de la République serving Basque specialties. *Piperade* (a spicy omelet) is a specialty. *Info*: 3rd/ Métro Arts-et-Métiers. 38 rue Réaumur. Tel. 01/42.72.69.25. Closed Sat, Sun & part of Aug. Moderate.

Bistro des Deux Théâtres
Affordable dining at this neighborhood bistro near the place de Clichy. Excellent *foie gras de canard* (fattened duck liver). *Info*: 9th/ Métro Trinité. 18 rue Blanche. Tel. 01/45.26.41.43. www.bistro-et-cie.fr. Moderate.

Bistrot Paul-Bert
A truly neighborhood bistro experience from its traditional decor

to its menu written on a blackboard. Extensive wine list for such a small place. *Info*: 11th/Métro Faidherbe-Chaligny. 18 rue Paul-Bert (See Right Bank Eats East Map). Tel. 01/43.72.24.01. Closed Sun & Mon. Moderate.

Bofinger
Beautiful glass-roofed *brasserie* with lots of stained glass and brass, located between the place des Vosges and the place de la Bastille. It's the oldest Alsatian *brasserie* in Paris, and still serves traditional dishes like *choucroute* (sauerkraut) and large platters of shellfish. *Info*: 4th/Métro Bastille. 5 rue de la Bastille (See Right Bank Eats East Map). Tel. 01/42.72.87.82. www.bofingerparis.com. Open daily until 1 am. Moderate. Across the street and less expensive is **Le Petit Bofinger**, 6 rue de la Bastille, Tel. 01/42.72.05.23.

La Boulangerie
A classic French bistro with a beautiful mosaic floor in a former bakery in the Ménilmontant area near Père-Lachaise cemetery. *Info*: 20th/Métro Ménilmontant. 15 rue des Panoyaux (See Right Bank Eats East Map). Tel. 01/43.58.45.45. Closed Sat (lunch) & Sun. Moderate.

Brasserie Flo
Alsatian food and Parisian atmosphere at this 1886 *brasserie*, on a passageway in an area not frequented by tourists. Jam-packed with some of the strangest people you'll see in Paris, and getting there is half the fun. Open daily until 1:30 a.m. *Info*: 10th/Métro Château d'Eau. 7 cour des Petites-Écuries (enter from 63 rue du Fg-St-Denis). Tel. 01/47.70.13.59. www.floparis.com. Moderate.

Chardenoux
Traditional Parisian cooking in the Bastille/République. This small and friendly restaurant has been in business for almost 100 years. *Info*: 11th/Métro Charonne. 1 rue Jules-Vallès and 23 rue Chanzy. (See Right Bank Eats East Map). Tel. 01/43.71.49.52. Closed Sat (lunch), Sun & part of Aug. Moderate.

Chez Paul
A favorite bistro in Paris. Never a bad meal (try the rabbit), and ask to eat upstairs. The service can be very Parisian, if you know

what I mean. *Info*: 11th/Métro Bastille or Ledru-Rollin. 13 rue de Charonne (See Right Bank Eats East Map). Tel. 01/47.00.34.57. Moderate.

La Cordonnerie
Just behind the place Vendôme, this tiny and friendly family-run restaurant serves classic French cuisine in a building dating back to the 1640s. *Info*: 1st/Métro Pyramides or Tuileries. 20 rue St-Roch. Tel. 01/42.60.17.42. Closed Sat & Sun. Moderate.

L'Enoteca
Attractive Italian wine bar/bistro in the Marais. It has one of the largest Italian wine selections in Paris. Delicious *risotto*. *Info*: 4th/Métro St-Paul. 25 rue Charles V (at rue St-Paul). Tel. 01/42.78.91.44. Closed part of Aug. www.enoteca.fr. Moderate.

Au Gamin de Paris
Small Marais bar/restaurant serving Parisian specialties. We've never had a bad meal here. Fun crowd. *Info*: 4th/Métro Saint-Paul. 51 rue Vieille du Temple. Tel. 01/42.78.97.24. Moderate.

Le Grand Colbert
Housed in a restored historic building, serving fine traditional *brasserie* cuisine. Known for its seafood tray. This stunning restaurant was featured in the movie *Something's Gotta Give*. *Info*: 2nd/Métro Bourse. 2 rue Vivienne (near the Place des Victoires). Tel. 01/42.86.87.88. Closed part of Aug. Moderate.

Aux Lyonnais
This beautiful century-old bistro has been recently renovated and serves the cuisine of Lyon. The wine of choice is Beaujolais. *Info*: 2nd/Métro Bourse. 32 rue St-Marc. Tel. 01/42.96.65.04. Closed Sat (lunch), Sun & Mon. Moderate.

Nos Ancêtres les Gaulois
Sit with other tourists. The waiters are humorously rude. The

food is not great and the menu is very limited. Definitely not for everyone. It's more of an experience than a dining experience. Get reservations. *Info*: 4th/Métro Pont Marie. 39 rue Saint-Louis-en-l'Île. www.nosancetreslesgaulois.com. Tel. 01/46.33.66.07. Moderate.

Au Petit Riche

This classic bistro serves specialties of the Loire Valley with a Parisian twist. Try the *civet* (game stew). *Info*: 9th/Métro Le Peletier. 25 rue Le Peletier (at rue Rossini). Tel. 01/47.70.68.68. www.aupetitriche.com. Closed Sun. Moderate.

Terminus Nord

What a great way to arrive in (or depart from) Paris! This large, bustling *brasserie* near the Gare du Nord is just so Parisian with its mahogany bar, polished wood and beveled glass. Seafood platters, *bouillabaisse* and duck breast are the featured dishes. Open daily until 1 a.m. *Info*: 10th/Métro Gare du Nord. 23 rue de Dunkerque. Tel. 01/42.85.05.15. www.terminusnord.com. Moderate.

Aux Trois Petits Cochons

Lively, friendly and gay (in every sense of the word) bistro in the Montorgueil quarter. Excellent *blanquette de veau* (veal stew). *Info*: 2nd/Métro Etienne Marcel. 31 rue Tiquetonne. Tel. 01/42.33.39.69. www.auxtroispetitscochons.fr. Open daily. No lunch. Moderate.

Willi's Wine Bar

British owners serving specialties with Mediterranean influences. A great wine list, and a favorite of many travelers to Paris. *Info*: 1st/Métro Bourse. 13 rue des Petits-Champs. Tel. 01/42.61.05.09. www.williswinebar.com. Closed Sun. Moderate.

INEXPENSIVE

Bistrot de l'Oulette

Small bistro in the Marais (near the place des Vosges) featuring the specialties of Southwest France (especially *confit*). It was formerly known as Baracane. *Info*: 4th/ Métro Bastille. 38 rue des Tournelles (See Right Bank Eats East Map). Tel. 01/42.71.43.33. www.l-oulette.com. Closed Sat (lunch) & Sun. Inexpensive-Moderate.

Chartier
Traditional Paris soup kitchen with affordable prices. The *tripes à la mode de Caen* is a frequent special of the day (I passed on that). Lots of tourists, and you may be seated with strangers which you'll really enjoy; it's a great way to meet people. Expect to wait in line. *Info*: 9th/Métro Grands Boulevards. 7 rue du Faubourg-Montmartre. Tel. 01/47.70.86.29. No reservations. Open daily. Inexpensive.

Chez Grisette
Delightful bistro in the heart of Montmartre. A real find. Start with *terrine e campagne* (pork-and-liver pâté). The friendly, English-speaking owner manages to take care of all the 24 people she can squeeze into her small bistro. *Info*: 18th/Métro Abbesses or Pigalle. 14 rue Houdon (see Montmartre Map). Tel. 01/42.62.04.80. www.chez-grisette.fr. Closed Sat & Sun. No lunch. Inexpensive-Moderate.

Le Hangar
Nothing fancy about this bistro serving classic French food near the Pompidou Center. Good food at reasonable prices. Excellent *gâteau au chocolat* (chocolate cake). *Info*: 3rd/Métro Rambuteau. 12 impasse Berthaud (off of rue Beaubourg). Tel. 01/42.74.55.44. Closed Sun, Mon & Aug. No credit cards. Inexpensive-Moderate.

Juvenile's
Around the corner from Willi's Wine Bar, this inexpensive, unpretentious wine bar serves light meals and has a large and interesting wine selection. Friendly and fun. *Info*: 1st/Métro Bourse. 47 rue de Richelieu. Tel. 01/42.97.46.49. Closed Sun. Inexpensive-Moderate.

Soprano
Overlooking the lovely place St-Catherine in the Marias (there are several other restaurants here), this unpretentious restaurant serves authentic Italian dishes. Welcoming staff and kid friendly. *Info*: 4th/Métro St-Paul. 5 rue Caron. Tel. 01/42.72.37.21. Inexpensive-Moderate.

Paris's Best Cafés

You have not experienced Paris unless you visit one of its many cafés. Parisians still stop by their local café to meet friends, read the newspaper or just watch the world go by. You should too. It doesn't matter if you order an expensive glass of wine or just a coffee because no one will hurry you. Sitting at a café in Paris is not only a great experience, but also one of the best bargains. If you're watching your euros, you can order and have your drink at the counter. You'll pay less as there's no service charge.

Café Beaubourg
Looking onto the Centre Pompidou and packed with an artsy crowd. The bathrooms are worth the trip. *Info*: 4th/Métro Rambuteau. 100 rue Saint-Martin. Tel. 01/48.87.63.96. Open daily 8am to 1pm. (Sat & Sun until 2am).

Café de Flore
Another famous café and a favorite of tourists and Parisians alike (next door to Les Deux Magots). *Info*: 6th/Métro Saint-Germain-des-Prés. 172 boulevard. Saint-Germain-des-Prés. Tel. 01/45.48.55.26. Open daily 7:30am. to 1:30am.

Café de la Paix
Famous café (not really known for its food). Popular with tourists. Another spot for outdoor people-watching (and the inside is beautiful). *Info*: 9th/Métro Opéra. 12 boulevard des

Capucines (place de l'Opéra). Tel. 01/40.07.30.20. Open daily 7am to midnight.

Café Les Deux Magots

If you're a tourist, you'll fit right in at one of Hemingway's favorite spots. We don't really recommend that you eat here (there is a limited menu), but have a drink and enjoy the great people-watching. *Info*: 6th/Métro Saint-Germain-des-Prés. 6 place Saint-Germain-des-Prés. Tel. 01/45.48.55.25. Open daily 7:30am to 1am.

Café L'Été en Pente Douce

Interesting and picturesque café near Sacré-Coeur. Take a break here before you climb the steps to Sacré-Coeur! *Info*: 18th/Métro Château-Rouge. 23 rue Muller. Tel. 01/42.64.02.67. Open daily noon to 3pm and 7pm to midnight.

Café Marly

This café overlooks the pyramid at the Louvre and no place in Paris has a better setting. Standard bistro fare served by waiters in suits. It is a great place for a relaxing lunch or you can come here after dinner and end your day with a glass of champagne. Definitely worth the cost! *Info*: 1st/Métro Musée du Louvre/ Palais-Royal. 93 rue de Rivoli. Tel. 01/49.26.06.60. Open daily 8am to 2am.

8. BEST ACTIVITIES

This chapter covers the best activities of this vibrant city: **shopping**, **nightlife**, and **sports and recreation**. You'll find great stores unique to Paris, fun bars and nightclubs, and suggestions for active travelers.

SHOPPING

Shops in Paris are more formal than at home. Always greet the person in a store with *bonjour madame* or *bonjour m'sieur* when entering.

Shopping Mania on and near the rue du Bac
There's shopping here for every interest. You'll find over 100 antique shops on rue du Bac, rue de Lille and rue de l'Université in the Carré Rive Gauche (between St-Germain-des-Prés and the Musée d'Orsay). The strangest shopping in Paris can be found at **Deyrolle** at 46 rue du Bac. You have to see this quirky taxidermy and household-goods shop to believe it.

Looking for clothes, shoes and accessories? Head to nearby rue de Grenelle, home to many **fashionable shoe shops**. For diverse shopping (everything from umbrellas to books), head east on boulevard St-Germain-des-Prés. Note: Many shops are closed on Sundays and Mondays. *Info*: Take the métro to the rue du Bac stop.

AMERICAN GOODS
The Real McCoy
Missing those potato chips and Oreos you eat at home? Then visit this American grocery store in the heart of the 7th arrondissement.

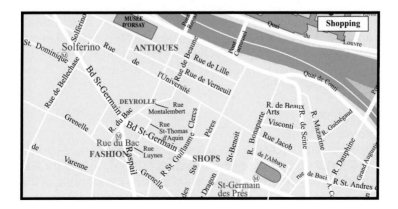

You'll find hundreds of grocery items from the United States, along with over-stuffed sandwiches and baked goods. *Info*: 7th/ Métro École Militaire. 194 rue de Grenelle. Tel. 01/45.56.98.82. Open daily 10am-10pm.

Breakfast in America
Tired of croissants? If you're homesick for an American breakfast, you can pretend you're in an American diner and be served eggs, hash browns and coffee (they sometimes even have French toast on the menu). *Info*: 5th/Métro Cardinal Lemoine. 17 rue des Écoles. Tel. 01/43.54.50.28. Open daily 8:30am-11pm.

ANTIQUES
Village St-Paul
An attractive passageway with cobblestone courtyards and interesting shops, especially antique shops. *Info*: 4th/Métro St-Paul. 23-27 rue St-Paul. Open Thu-Mon 11am-7pm.

Le Louvre des Antiquaires
You'll find 250 antique shops at the arcades along rue de Rivoli facing the Louvre. You can go inside and visit all of these shops (not just enter from rue de Rivoli). There are Art Deco objects, antiquities, furniture and art. *Info*: 2nd/Métro Palais Royal. Place du Palais-Royal. Open Tue-Sat 11am-7pm.

ART – Folk/Naive
Halle St-Pierre/Musée d'Art Max Fourny
The **Halle St-Pierre** is a former 19th-century market hall with exhibit space, a café and shops. The **Musée d'Art Max Fourny** displays temporary exhibitions of folk/naive art from around the world. A must for folk-art aficionados. *Info*: 18th/Métro Anvers. 2 rue Ronsard (at the bottom of the hill on the right as you face the Sacred Heart Basilica). Tel. 01/42.58.72.89. Open daily 10am-6pm. Admission: €6.

AUCTIONS
Drouot-Richelieu
This huge auction house has stood on the corner of rues Drouot and Rossini since the mid-1800s. An "exposition" of items for sale is held the day before and from 11am to noon the morning of the

auction. Auction sales usually begin at 2pm. You can inspect everything from paintings and furniture to wine and ancient objects in the auction house's sixteen rooms. A truly interesting experience and, if the price is right, you may come home with a little bit of Paris. *Info*: 9th/Métro Richelieu-Drouot. 9 Rue Drouot. Tel. 01/48.00.20.20. Open Mon-Sat 11am-6pm. Admission: Free.

BOOKS – English
Shakespeare and Company
This famous bookstore is named after the publishing house that

first released James Joyce's *Ulysses*. Hemingway and Fitzgerald were patrons. It's a favorite hangout for expatriates from English-speaking countries. Poetry readings on Monday evenings (if you like that sort of thing). *Info*: 5th/Métro St-Michel. 37 rue de la Bûcherie. Tel. 01/43.25.40.93. Open daily noon to midnight.

Les Bouquinistes
These little green stands sell everything from replicas of the Eiffel Tower to old magazines. It's great fun to browse through French posters, postcards, and books. You can find inexpensive and

interesting souvenirs. *Info*: Along the Seine River. They are usually open around 10am and close around 6pm.

CHEESE SHOPS
– *Fromageries*
Alléosse
Cheese is like gold to the French. Charles de Gaulle is reported to have said, "How can anyone govern a nation that has 246 different kinds of cheese?" This pretty cheese

shop serves rare cheeses from throughout France. It's located on a busy market street. *Info*: 17th/Métro Ternes. 13 rue Poncelet. Tel. 01/46.22.50.45. Closed Mon.

Barthélemy
This small cheese shop on the Left Bank is where Parisians shop for their cheese. When you walk in, you're overtaken by the intense smell of some of the best cheeses available in France. *Info*: 7th/Métro Rue du Bac. 51 rue de Grenelle. Tel. 01/45.48.56.75. Closed Sun & Mon.

CLOTHES
Colette
Open for ten years, this cutting-edge store with lots of attitude sells designer clothing, shoes, perfume, makeup and even art and books. There's a basement café/water bar. *Info*: 1ˢᵗ/Métro Tuileries. 213 rue St-Honoré. Tel. 01/55.35.33.90. Open Mon-Sat 11am-7pm. www.colette.fr.

Le Bon Marché
The first department store in the city is known for its designer-clothes departments. *Info*: 7ᵗʰ/Métro Sèvres-Babylone. 38 rue de Sèvres. Tel. 01/44.39.80.00. Open Mon-Fri 9:30am-7pm, Thu 10am-9pm, Sat 9:30am-8pm.

L'Habilleur
Last season's designer clothes (both men and women) at seriously reduced prices. *Info*: 3ʳᵈ/Métro St-Sébastien-Froissart. 44 rue de Poitou. Tel. 01/48.87.77.12. Open Mon-Sat noon-8pm.

Zara
A Spanish chain of clothing stores featuring reasonably priced knock-offs of runway fashions for men, women and children. Several locations throughout the city. *Info*: 8ᵗʰ/Métro F.D.-Roosevelt. 44 ave. des Champs-Élysées (main store). Tel. 01/45.61.52.80. www.zara.com.

Vintage
This small vintage clothing store has an interesting collection of purses, clothes, shoes and hats that some Parisian wore at one

time or another. *Info*: 4th/Métro St-Paul. 32 rue des Rosiers. Tel. 01/40.27.04.98. Open daily 11am-10pm.

CRYSTAL & PORCELAIN

Baccarat

Crystal boutique and museum. The setting is appropriate, a 1900 stone mansion, with dozens of crystal chandeliers (all for sale for over $100,000, in case you're interested). Across the street is the **Le Cristal Room Baccarat** restaurant (Tel. 01/40.22.11.10. Closed Sunday. Reservations required). *Info*: 16th/Métro Boissière. 11 place des Etats-Unis. Tel. 01/40.22.11.22. Open Mon-Sat 10am-7pm. Boutiques also at 11 place de la Madeleine (8th/Métro Madeleine), 17 rue de la Paix (2nd/Métro Opéra), and 3 place Général Koenig (17th/Métro Porte Maillot).

Limoges-Unic/Madronet

The Rue de Paradis is the street to walk down for crystal, ceramic and porcelain shops, especially this shop. *Info*: 10th/Métro Gare de l'Est. 34 and 58 rue de Paradis. Tel. 01/47.70.34.59. Open Mon-Sat 11am-6pm.

DEPARTMENT STORES

Monoprix

Parisians head to this supermarket and discount department store. There are locations throughout Paris. The stores are particularly known for their budget-priced, quality cosmetics. *Info*: Most are open Mon-Sat 9am-9pm.

Galeries Lafayette

Opened in 1894. You'll find designer clothes, a wonderful food hall and a free view of Paris from the 7th floor. *Info*: 9th/Métro Chaussée d'Antin. 40 blvd. Haussmann. Tel. 01/42.82.34.56. Open Mon-Sat 9:30am-7:30pm (Thu until 9pm). *See photo on page 194.*

Au Printemps

Opened in 1864. Here, you'll find designer clothing, household goods and furniture. The tea room on the 6th floor has a stained-glass ceiling. *Info*: 9th/Métro Havre-Caumartin. 64 blvd. Haussmann. Tel. 01/42.82.57.87. Open Mon-Sat 9:30am-7pm (Thu until 10pm).

Le Bon Marché
The first department store in the city. Gustave Eiffel, who designed the Eiffel Tower, had a hand in its design. Best known for **La Grande Épicerie**, the ultimate grocery store. *Info*: 7th/Métro Sèvres-Babylone. 38 rue de Sèvres. Tel. 01/44.39.80.00. Open Mon-Fri 9:30am-7pm, Thu 10am-9pm, Sat 9:30am-8pm.

BHV
The Bazar de l'Hôtel de Ville has everything from household goods to clothing. It's known for its interesting domestic-goods department. *Info*: 4th/Métro Hôtel de Ville. 52-64 rue de Rivoli. Tel. 01/42.74.90.00. Open Mon-Sat 9:30am-7:30pm (Wed until 9pm).

DRUGSTORE
Publicis Drugstore
Opened in 1958 and recently renovated, this is not just a drugstore on a famous street. You'll also find boutiques, a newsstand, wine shop, specialty-food market and restaurants. *Info*: 8th/Métro Champs-Élysées. 133 bis Avenue des Champs-Élysées. Tel. 01/44.43.79.00. Open Mon-Fri 8am-2am, Sat, Sun & holidays 10am-2am.

FLEA MARKETS
Clignancourt Flea Market
This is the **Marché aux Puces** ("flea market"), the most famous in Paris. When you get off at the métro stop, just follow the crowds. Work your way through the junk on the outskirts of the market (watch your wallet) until you find the interesting antique dealers around rue des Rosiers and avenue Michelet. You can find all sorts of small souvenirs to take home. If you get hungry, there are cheap snack stands and a few good restaurants. *Info*: 18th/Métro Porte de Clignancourt (cross boulevard Ney). Open Sat-Mon 9am-7pm.

Some think the **Marché aux Puces de la Porte de Vanves** is better for purchases, but definitely has less atmosphere. *Info*: 14th/ Métro Porte de Vanves. Avenue Georges-Lafenestre. Open Sat-Mon 6:30pm-4:30pm.

FOOD SHOPS

Christian Constant

Chocolates made with ingredients from around the world. *Info*: 6th/Métro Saint-Placide. 37 rue d'Assas. Tel. 01/53.63.15.15. Open Mon-Fri 8:30am-9pm, Sat-Sun 8am-8:30pm.

La Maison du Chocolat

Every chocolate lover should visit. *Info*: 8th/Métro Ternes 225 rue du Faubourg-St-Honoré. Tel. 01/42.27.39.44. Open Mon-Sat 10am-7pm, Sun 10am-1pm. There are also shops at: 52 rue François 1er (8th/Métro Franklin-D.-Roosevelt), 8 boulevard de la Madeleine (9th/Métro Madeleine), 19 rue de Sèvres (6th/Métro Sèvres Babylone), and 89 avenue Ramond Poincaré (16th/Métro Dauphine).

Patrick Roger

Patrick Roger is a young chocolate maker from the town of Sceaux near Paris. His friendly shop on the boulevard St-Germain-des-Prés has excellent chocolates packaged in green boxes that make great gifts and are easy to pack to take home. *Info*: 6th/Métro Odéon. 108 boulevard St-Germain-des-Prés. Tel. 01/43.29.38.42. Open Tue-Sat 10:30am-7:30pm.

Stohrer

The Parisian favorite of *baba au rhum* (spongecake soaked in rum) was invented at this *pâtisserie* in the Montorgueil quarter. When available, try a *macaron*. It isn't the sticky coconut version, but two almond-meringue cookies, flavored with vanilla, chocolate, coffee, pistachio, or other flavor, stuck together with butter cream. *Info*: 2nd/Métro Les Halles. 51 rue Montorgueil. Tel. 01/42.33.38.20. Open daily 7:30am-10:30pm. Closed part of Aug.

A La Mère de Famille

The oldest *confiserie* (candy shop) in Paris (since 1761). *Info*: 9th/Métro Le Peletier or Cadet. 35 rue du Faubourg-Montmartre. Tel. 01/47.70.83.69. Closed Sun, Mon & Aug.

A L'Étoile d'Or
This incredible store, near the tacky sex shops of the Pigalle area, has some of the best candy concoctions you could ever imagine. *Info*: 9th/Métro Pigalle. 30 rue Fontaine. Tel. 01/48.74.59.55. Closed Mon (morning) & Sun.

Albert Ménès
Gourmet food shop that specializes in food from the provinces. *Info*: 8th/Métro Madeleine or St-Augustin. 41 boulevard Malesherbes. Tel. 01/42.66.95.63. Closed Sun & mid-July to mid-Aug.

Gourmet Lafayette
This department store has a huge gourmet-food section. *Info*: 8th/Métro Chaussée-d'Antin. 40 boulevard Haussmann (in the Galeries Lafayette department store). Tel. 01/42.82.34.56. Closed Sun.

La Grande Épicerie
The ultimate grocery store (with wine cellar and carry-out). *Info*: 7th/Métro Sèvres Babylone. 38 rue Sèvres (in the Le Bon Marché department store). Tel. 01/44.39.81.00. Closed Sun.

Oliviers & Co.
Olive oils from around the Mediterranean at several lovely shops. *Info*: 2nd/90 rue Montorgueil, 4th/47 rue Vieille du Temple, 4th/81 rue St Louis en l'Île, 5th/128 rue Mouffetard. 6th/28 rue de Buci, 7th/44 rue Cler, 15th/85 rue du Commerce, and 17th/8 bis rue de Lévis.

GIFTS
Les Touristes
You can always find something unusual at this Marais boutique filled with interesting things the owners have collected during their trips around the world. Great place to buy gifts to bring home. *Info*: 4th/Métro Hôtel de Ville or Rambuteau. 17 rue des Blancs-Manteaux. Tel. 01/42.72.10.84. Closed Sun.

Plaques & Pots
Those metal signs found throughout Paris (everything from

street signs to "beware of dog" signs) can be found at this tiny shop with a friendly owner. Unique gift idea. *Info*: 1ˢᵗ/Métro Les Halles. 12 rue de la Ferronnerie. Tel. 01/42.36.21.72. Open Mon 2pm-6:30pm, Tue-Sat 10:30am-6:30pm. www.plaquesetpots.fr.

HOME ACCESSORIES
Le Monde Sauvage
Home accessories, the Parisian way. Everything from bed linens to crystal chandeliers. *Info*: 6ᵗʰ/Métro Odéon. 11 rue de l'Odéon. Tel. 01/43.25.60.34. Closed Mon (morning) and Sun.

Viaduc des Arts
Fifty workshops in a restored train viaduct feature interesting furniture, pottery, dishes and linen. *Info*: 12ᵗʰ/Métro Gare de Lyon. Along avenue Daumesnil. Open Mon-Sat 11am-7pm.

JEWELRY
Dary's
If you're a jewelry lover or looking for jewelry to bring home (from antique to modern second-hand jewelry), come here! *Info*: 1ˢᵗ/Métro Tuileries. 362 rue St-Honoré. Tel. 01/42.60.95.23. Open Mon-Fri 10am-6pm, Sat noon-6pm.

KITCHENWARE
Lenôtre
Café, kitchen shop (everything from pots and pans to wine) and cooking school all in the elegant glass-and-stone Pavillon Élysée. Lenôtre has sixteen other pastry shops in Paris. *Info*: 8th/Métro Champs-Élysées – Clemenceau. 10 avenue des Champs-Élysées. Tel. 01/42.65.85.10.

A. Simon
This kitchenware shop is where the chefs shop. You can fill your own kitchen with pans, glassware and some stuff you find only in bistros (like paper doilies and chalkboards). *Info*: 2ⁿᵈ/Métro Les Halles. 48 rue Montmartre. Tel. 01/42.33.71.65. Open Tue-Sat 9am-6:30pm, Mon 1:30pm-6:30pm.

MALLS
Le Carrousel du Louvre
You'll find a shopping mall with over 45 stores below the Louvre. There's also a restaurant court here. An inverted glass pyramid drops down into the center of the mall. Look familiar? It was also designed by I.M. Pei, who designed the famous pyramid entry to the Louvre. *Info*: 1st/Métro Palais-Royal. 99 rue de Rivoli. Open daily 10am-8pm.

Forum des Halles
Unattractive underground mall (and métro and bus station) where Paris's youth hang out in droves. Chain stores, a swimming pool and movie-theatre complex are all here. Skip it! The park above, with its Renaissance fountain, the **Fontaine des Innocents,** is quite nice. *Info*: 1st/Métro Les Halles.

PASSAGES
In the 1800s, there were 137 glass-roofed shopping arcades (*passages*) in Paris. Only 24 remain. The oldest, dating back to 1800, is

Passage des Panoramas, 11 blvd. Montmartre (known for its stamps). Nearby are **Passage Verdeau,** 4-6 rue de la Grange Batelière, and **Passage Jouffroy,** 12 blvd. Montmartre. *Passages* are luminous and practical. The glass roofs not only admit light, but shelter shoppers from rain. *Info*: 2nd/Métro Grands Boulevards.

SHOES
Budget name-brand shoes? You'll find last season's shoe collections at the crowded discount stores on **rue Meslay** in the République area. *Info*: 3rd/Métro République.

STAMPS
Marché aux Timbres
Stamps from all over the world and vintage postcards can be found at the stamp market off the Champs-Élysées at Rond-

Point. Made famous in the 1963 movie *Charade* featuring Audrey Hepburn and Cary Grant, which was filmed almost entirely in Paris. *Info*: 8th/Métro Champs-Élysées or Franklin-D.-Roosevelt. Off of the Champs-Élysées at Rond-Point/near the junction of avenues Gabriel and Marigny. Open Thu-Sun 10am to 5pm.

TAXIDERMY
Deyrolle
A taxidermy shop "stuffed" with everything from snakes to baby elephants to zebras. Also on display are collections of butterflies, shells and minerals from all over the world. Kids seem to love this place. You have to go upstairs! The shop also sells planters, clothes and other household items (some modeled on the stuffed animals). Very quirky! *Info*: 7th/Métro Rue du Bac. 46 rue du Bac. Tel: 01/42.22.30.07. Closed Sun.

UPSCALE SHOPPING AREAS
place Vendôme
This elegant square is the home of a 144-foot column honoring Napoléon. The column is faced with bronze from 1,200 melted cannons from Austrian and Russian armies. That's Napoléon on top dressed as Julius Caesar. Although the Ministry of Justice is here, most notice the luxury Ritz Hôtel and the expensive shops nearby, especially on rue St-Honoré. You'll find world-famous jewelers  here, and great shopping for those with lots of disposable income. *Info*: 1st/Métro Tuileries. Between the Jardin des Tuileries and the Opéra Garnier.

Rue du Faubourg-St-Honoré
In the 1700s, this street was home to the richest residents of Paris. Today, it's home (along with nearby **avenue Montaigne**) to designer boutiques. Window-shopping for the rich. *Info*: 8th/ Métro Concorde (rue du Faubourg-St-Honoré) and 8th/Métro Franklin-D. Roosevelt (avenue Montaigne). Just a few shops are:

- Prada, 6 rue du Faubourg-St-Honoré and 10 avenue Montaigne
- Hermès, 24 rue du Faubourg-St-Honoré
- Yves Saint Laurent, 32 and 38 rue du Faubourg-St-Honoré
- Christian Lacroix, 73 rue du Faubourg-St-Honoré
- Christian Dior, 30 avenue Montaigne
- Chanel, 40 avenue Montaigne
- Marni, 57 avenue Montaigne

WINE SHOPS
Galerie Vivienne
Duck into this elegant and beautiful gallery of luxurious shops. While here, check out **Legrand Filles et Fils,** Tel. 01/42.60.07.12. This wine shop and bar has been run by the Legrand family for over three generations. Be sure to check out the cork-covered ceiling. The gallery leads into the **Galerie Colbert**. *Info*: 2nd/ Métro Bourse. 4 rue des Petits-Champs. Open Tue-Sat 10am-7pm, Mon 11am-7pm.

Lavinia
The largest wine shop in Paris with 2000 foreign wines, 3000 French wines and 1000 spirits, priced from €3 to €3600. Drink any bottle from the shop at the wine bar. Lunch served with wine, of course. No dinner. *Info*: 1st/Métro Madeleine. 3-5 boulevard de la Madeleine. Tel. 01/42.97.20.20. Open Mon-Sat 10am-8pm.

Les Caves Taillevent
This wine shop is associated with the well-known Taillevent restaurant and is said to have over 500,000 bottles of wine starting at around €5. You'll be amazed at the cost of some selections. *Info*: 8th/Métro Charles-de-Gaulle-Étoile or Saint-Philippe-du-Roule. 199 rue du Faubourg-Saint-Honoré. Tel. 01/45.61.14.09. Open Tue-Sat 9am-7:30pm, Mon 2pm-7:30pm.

Nicolas
Over 200 wine stores located throughout Paris. The main one is in the 8th/Métro Madeleine at 31 place de la Madeleine. *Info*: Tel. 01/44.51.90.22. Open Mon-Sat 9:30pm-8pm. www.nicolas-wines.com.

NIGHTLIFE & ENTERTAINMENT

From bars and cabarets, to movies, jazz, concerts, dance performances and more, Paris has a terrific nightlife scene.

BARS

Barrio Latino
Four-story bar, restaurant and nightclub. There are several bars in the complex and balconies surround the dance floor with music heavy on salsa and samba. *Info*: 12th/Métro Bastille. 46-48 rue Fbg. St-Antoine. Tel. 01/55.78.84.75. Open daily noon-2am.

Buddha Bar
Asian-themed, trendy bar known for its music. Expensive cocktails and can be a little touristy at times. *Info*: 8th/Métro Concorde. 8 rue Boissy d'Anglais. Tel. 01/53.05.90.00. www.buddahbar.com.

Culture Bière
Bar, café and boutique selling everything from glassware to beer-based skin products. It's owned by Heineken. You won't find any French wine here! *Info*: 8th/Métro Franklin-D. Roosevelt. 65 avenue des Champs-Élysées. Tel. 01/42.56.88.88. Open daily for lunch and dinner. www.culturebiere.com

Le Dokhan
An elegant champagne bar where you can enjoy it by the flute or by the bottle. *Info*: 16th/Métro Trocadéro. 117 rue Lauriston (located in Trocadéro Dokhan's Hôtel). Tel. 01/53.65.66.99. Open daily (evenings only).

Hemingway's
You can visit one of Ernest Hemingway's favorite spots at this bar (now named for him) at the swanky Hôtel Ritz. Dress up and expect to hand out quite a few euros for your drinks (cocktails

cost €23). *Info*: 1ˢᵗ/Métro Opéra. 15 place Vendôme. Tel. 01/ 43.16.33.65. Open Mon-Sat 6:30pm-2am.

Le Trésor
Cocktails served both inside and outside at tables along this lovely, flowered street in the heart of the Marais. Great people-watching. *Info*: 4th/Métro Hôtel de Ville or Saint-Paul. 5-7 rue du Trésor (off of rue Vieille du Temple) Tel. 01/42.71.35.17.

CABARET
Le Lido
Elaborate costumes, special effects, sixty Bluebell Girls, the Lido Boy dancers and even ice skating make for an interesting evening at this famous cabaret. It's not for everyone, but people have been enjoying the show since 1946. *Info*: 8ᵗʰ/Métro Champs-Élysées. 116 bis avenue des Champs-Élysées. Tel. 01/40.76.56.10. Admission: €80-100, €140-200 (with dinner).

Moulin Rouge
You've seen the movie, now see the cancan. Originally a red windmill, this dance hall has been around since 1889. It's without  a doubt the most famous cabaret in the world. Toulouse-Lautrec memorialized the Moulin Rouge in his paintings. Looking for a little bit of Vegas? You'll find it here. *Info*: 18ᵗʰ/Métro Blanche. 82 boulevard de Clichy. Tel. 01/53.09.82.82. Shows nightly at 9pm and 11pm. Admission: €87 (11pm show with half bottle of champagne). €140-170 (7pm dinner followed by 9pm show). www.moulinrouge.fr.

FILM
Parisians are huge film buffs. There are cinemas throughout the city. If a movie is marked with a "vo", this means "*version*

originale" or in the original language. So, if it's an American movie, the movie will be subtitled in French (so you'll be able to hear the original movie). If the movie is marked with a "vf", this means *"version française"* and the movie will be dubbed in French.

Cinémathèque Français

Daily film classics and a collection of movie memorabilia housed in an interesting Frank Gehry building. *Info*: 12th/Métro Bercy. 51 rue de Bercy. Tel 01/71.19.33.33. Open Mon, Wed and Fri noon-7pm; Thu noon-10pm, Sat and Sun 10am-8pm. www.cinematheque.fr.

GAY

Paris has long had an active gay community, and has even elected a gay mayor. The **Marais** is the center of gay life. The largest concentration of gay bars, clubs, restaurants and shops is located between the Hôtel de Ville and Rambuteau métro stops. For information on gay establishments, visit www.gay-paris.com. For apartment rentals, visit www.mycityflat.com, Tel. 01/42.78.01.58. For current events, try www.agenda2x.com (partially in English).

Here are a few establishments:
- **Unity**, 3rd/Métro Rambuteau, 176 rue St-Martin, Tel. 01/42.72.70.59 (bar for women)
- **Open Café**, 4th/Métro Hôtel de Ville, 17 rue des Archives, Tel. 01/42.72.26.18 (bar/café for men)
- **Amnesia Café**, 4th/Métro Hôtel de Ville, 42 rue Vieille-du-Temple, Tel. 01/42.72.16.94 (bar/café for men and women)
- **Okawa**, 4th/Métro Hôtel de Ville, 40 rue Vieille-du-Temple, Tel. 01/48.04.30.69 (comfortable and quiet bar for men)
- **Le Central**, 4th/Métro Hôtel de Ville, 33 rue Vieille-du-Temple, Tel. 01/48.87.99.33 (long-standing bar for men with small hotel above)
- **Le Dépôt**, 3rd/ Métro Etienne Marcel, 10 rue aux Ours, Tel 01/44.54.96.96 (bar/dancing/cruising)
- **Aux Trois Petits Cochons**, 2nd/Métro Etienne Marcel, 31 rue Tiquetonne, Tel. 01/42.33.39.69 (restaurant)
- **Pig'z**, 2nd/Métro Etienne Marcel, 5 rue Marie Stuart, Tel. 01/42.33.05.89 (restaurant)

- **Stuart Friendly**, 2nd/ Métro Etienne Marcel, 16 rue Marie Stuart, Tel. 01/42.33.24.00 (coffee shop/café/restaurant)

IRISH PUB

Many Irish live in Paris. Irish pubs are popular not only with the Irish who are looking for a pint, but also with Parisians. Most Irish pubs feature live music (especially on the weekends). A favorite is **Quiet Man** at 5 rue des Haudriettes, 3rd/Métro Rambuteau, Tel. 01/48.04.42.77. Open daily 5pm-2am.

JAZZ

Parisians love jazz. There are several jazz clubs on rue des Lombards (1st/Métro Châtelet or Les Halles). Nothing gets going until after 9pm (if then). Take your pick:
- **Au Duc des Lombards** (number 42)
- **Le Basier Salé** (number 58)
- **Le Sunset/LeSunside** (number 60)

Franc Pinot is an intimate jazz club at 1 quai de Bourbon on the Île St-Louis (closed Sun and Mon).

MUSIC (CLASSICAL/OPERA)

You'll see posters all over advertising choral or orchestra concerts at bargain prices. Usually, these concerts are held in beautiful but lesser-known churches throughout Paris, and make for a wonderful evening before dinner.

Opéra Garnier

Built in 1875, this ornate opera house is now the showplace for both opera and dance. It's often referred to as the most opulent theater in the world. Chandeliers, marble stairways, red-velvet boxes, a ceiling painted by Chagall, and a facade of marble and sculpture all make this the perfect place for an elegant night out in Paris. There's also a museum cele-

Advance Tickets

Want to get **tickets to events before you leave home?** Globaltickets of New York, *www.globaltickets.com*, will mail tickets to you for the opera, symphony, special events and tourist attractions before you leave for Paris. There's about a 25% surcharge.

brating opera and dance over the years (Open daily 10am-5pm, Admission: €7). *Info*: 9th/Métro Opéra. place de l'Opéra. Tel. 08/92.89.90.90 (box office).

Opéra Bastille
Opened in 1989, this modern glass building hosts opera and symphony performances. *Info*: 11th/Métro Bastille. East end of rue St-Antoine. 08/92.89.90.90 (box office).

MUSIC (DANCE)
Batofar
Experience late-night Paris by dancing on a barge floating in the Seine River. Mostly 20-to 30-year-olds cram the club to dance to everything from techno to jazz. *Info*: 13th/Métro Quai de la Gare. 11 quai François Mauriac. Tel 01/53.60.17.30. Open Apr-Oct Tue-Sat 6pm-3am. Admission: €10-€20 (cover). www.batofar.org

Les Bains Douches
Techno and dance music at this late-night club (don't get here until well after midnight) located in a former Turkish bath. Large gay following. *Info*: Métro Etienne Marcel. 7 rue du Bourg-l'Abbé. Tel. 01/48.87.01.80. Open Tue-Sun. Admission: €20 (cover). www.lesbainsdouches.net.

Caveau de la Huchette
From classic rock and roll to jazz, thirtysomethings hit this medieval cellar on the Left Bank. *Info*: 5th/Métro St-Michel. 5 rue de la Huchette. Tel. 01/43.26.65.05. Open Mon-Sat at 9:30pm. www.caveaudelahuchette.fr.

MUSIC (FRENCH)
Au Lapin Agile
You'll likely hear French folk tunes coming out of this shuttered cottage at the
picturesque intersection of rue des Saules
and rue St-Vincent. It was once frequented by Picasso. Today, you'll sit at
small wooden tables and listen to
chansonniers (singers). Truly a Parisian
experience. *Info*: 18th/Métro Lamarck-

Caulaincourt. Intersection of rue des Saules and rue St-Vincent. Tel. 01/46.06.85.87. Open Tue-Sun 9pm-2am. Closed Mon. Admission: €24 (includes a drink). No credit cards. Reservations can be made at www.au-lapin-agile.com.

MUSIC (WORLD)
New Morning
This spartan music club (in the increasingly trendy 10th) is where you come to hear jazz, world music and folk. *Info*: 10th/Métro Château d'Eau. 7 rue des Petites-Écuries. Tel. 01/45.23.51.41. Open Mon-Sat 8pm-1:30am. Closed Sun.

SPA
L'Appartement 217
Need rejuvenation after that long flight? Try the ultimate Parisian spa. Facials (begin at €50), massage and beauty products. *Info*: 1st/Métro Tuileries. 217 rue St-Honoré. Reservations: Tel. 01/42.96.00.96. www.lappartement217.com.

SEX
place Pigalle
You come here for only one thing: sex. Littered with sex shops, this area was known as "Pig Alley" during World War II. During the day, neighborhood residents walking with their children and eating ice cream seem oblivious to all the sex shops, reminding us that this is, after all, just another Paris neighborhood. *Info*: 18th/ Métro Pigalle. Eastern end of boulevard de Clichy.

SPORTS & RECREATION

You can exercise more than your cultural and culinary appetite here in Paris: choose from boat rides, bike tours, indoor swimming, amusement parks, and more.

AMUSEMENT PARKS
Disneyland Paris
The biggest tourist attraction in France (even greater than the

Eiffel Tower), Disneyland Paris isn't much different than the Disney parks in the U.S. Main Street USA, Adventureland, Frontierland, Fantasyland and Discoveryland are all here. **Village Disney** is a free entertainment area with restaurants, bars and clubs. **Walt Disney Studios** (an interactive film studio) is next to Disneyland (separate admission charge). *Info*: Take the RER line A (from many métro stops such as Nation, Châtelet-Les Halles or Charles-de-Gaulle-

Étoile) to Marne-la Vallée/Chessy. 45-minute trip. Fare is €13 round-trip. Tel. 01/60.30.60.30. Open daily 10am-8pm. One-day admission to Disneyland is €30 for adults, €25 ages 3-1, under 3 free. Package deals available. www.disneylandparis.com.

Jardin d'Acclimatation

The northern 25 acres of the **Bois de Boulogne** is just the place for kids. You can take a ride on the yellow-and-green train to the amusement-park entrance from the Porte Maillot métro stop, which departs every 20 minutes (€1.25). Playgrounds, pony rides, a zoo, miniature golf course, bowling alleys, a hall of mirrors ...you get the picture. La Prévention Routière is probably the most interesting attraction. It's a miniature roadway where children drive small cars. Real police officers (*gendarmes*) teach kids to follow and obey stoplights and street signs. *Info*: 16th/ Métro Porte Maillot. Tel. 01/40.67.90.82. Open daily Jun-Sep 10am-7pm (Oct-May until 6pm). Admission: €3, under 3 free.

BIKE TOURS

Fat Tire Bike Tours

They offer four-hour day and night bike tours of Paris. There's also a seven-hour tour of Monet's House and Garden in Giverny and an eight-hour tour of Versailles. The guides speak English. *Info*: Reservations can be made online or by calling 01/56.58.10.54. www.fattirebiketoursparis.com.

Paris Charms & Secrets
This company hosts electric bike tours (no peddling!) to many Paris sights like the Eiffel Tower and Montmartre (where there are lots of hills). The trips are daily at 9:30am, 2:30pm and 8pm. The guides speak English and the trips last about four hours (three hours for the night trips). *Info*: Reserve online or by calling 01/40.29.00.00. Prices from €36 per person. www.parischarmssecrets.com.

BOAT TOURS
Batobus
This is a river-boat shuttle service with eight stops in central Paris near major tourist sights. You can get on and off as often as you

want. A great way to see the sights from the Seine River. *Info*: Tickets sold at eight stops along the River near the Eiffel Tower, Musée d'Orsay, St-Germain-des-Prés, Notre-Dame, Jardin des Plantes, Hôtel de Ville, Louvre, and Champs-Élysées. Tickets also sold at most tourist offices (including the airport). July and August 10am-7pm. Mid-Mar-May and Sep-Nov 10am-7pm. Feb-mid-Mar and Nov-Dec 10:30am-4:30pm. Does not operate in Jan except the first week. One-day pass €11, two consecutive days €13, five consecutive days €16.

PARKS (WALKING, JOGGING, RELAXING)
Bois de Boulogne
An enormous park (nearly 2,200 acres) open 24 hours a day (avoid it at night). Walking paths, lakes, a waterfall, an amusement park (see above), children's zoo and two horse racetracks are all here. **Parc de St-Cloud** is another less-crowded park at the western end of métro line 10 (Métro Boulogne/Pont de St-Cloud). Come here for fountains, flowers, ponds and tranquil walks. *Info*: On the western edge of the 16th/Métro Porte Dauphine.

Bois de Vincennes
Past the medieval castle, **Château de Vincennes** (Tel. 01/48.08.31.20, open daily. Admission: €6), is the **Bois de Vincennes**

(woods) containing a beautiful floral park, the **Parc Floral** (Tel. 01/55.94.20.20, open daily. Admission: €3). If you're interested in gardening, especially flowers, you'll enjoy viewing not only the seasonal flowers, but also the bamboo, bonsai, medicinal plants and ferns (all labeled with their latin names). *Info*: 12th/Métro Château de Vincennes. Eastern edge of Paris.

Jardin des Plantes
Another quiet park in Paris, especially known for its herb garden. The zoo here (the **Ménagerie**) is one of the oldest in the world. *Info*: 5th/Métro Jussieu or Monge. Off of the Quai St-Bernard, west of Gare d'Austerlitz. Tel. 01/40.79.30.00. Open daily 8am-6pm. Zoo open daily 9am-5pm. Admission: Free (gardens), €7 (zoo).

Parc des Buttes-Chaumont
Created in 1867 (from a former garbage dump), this peaceful park has artificial cliffs, streams, waterfalls and jogging paths. *Info*: 19th/Métro Botzaris. rue Manin. Open daily 9am-sunset. Admission: Free.

Parc Monceau
For a break from hectic Paris, stop in this beautiful park surrounded by 18th- and 19th-century mansions. *Info*: 8th/Métro Monceau. A few blocks northeast from the Arc de Triomphe down avenue Hoche and avenue Van Dyck.

SKATING
An ice skating rink is installed in front of the **Hôtel de Ville** (City Hall) in the winter. *Info*: 4th/Métro Hôtel de Ville.

TENNIS
Tenniseum Roland-Garros
Until recently, access to the Roland-Garros Stadium has been limited to spectators attending the French Open. The stadium is now open year-round with guided tours (some in English). A multimedia museum ("Tenniseum") is devoted to 500 years of tennis history. Visitors can watch 200 hours of tennis action, visit a huge library devoted solely to tennis, and kids can participate in workshops with their parents. A must for tennis lovers. *Info*:

16th/Métro Porte d'Auteuil. Tel. 01/47.43.48.48. 2 ave. Gordon-Bennett. Open 10am-6pm. Closed Mon. Admission: €8.

WATERPARK
Aquaboulevard
Kids will love this huge water park and sports center. Wave pools, water slides, tennis courts, golf range and a food court. No matter what your age or size, all men are required to wear speedo-type swimsuits. What's that all about? *Info*: 15th/Métro Porte de Versailles or Balard. 4 rue Louis-Armand. Tel. 01/40.60.10.00. Open daily 7am-midnight. Admission: €20 (family passes at reduced price).

12. PRACTICAL MATTERS

GETTING TO PARIS

AIRPORTS/ARRIVAL
Paris has two international airports: **Charles de Gaulle (Roissy)** and **Orly**. An Air France shuttle operates between the airports every 30 minutes. The trip takes up to 75 minutes and costs €13.

At Charles de Gaulle, a free shuttle bus connects Aérogare 1 (used by most foreign carriers) with Aérogare 2 (used primarily by Air France). This bus also drops you off at the Roissy train station. Line B departs every 15 minutes from 5:30am to midnight to major métro stations. The cost is €8.10. Connecting métro lines will take you to your final destination. The train stops at Gare du Nord, Châtelet-Les Halles, St-Michel and Luxembourg stations. The trip takes about 35 minutes to Châtelet-Les Halles.

The **Roissy buses** run every 15 minutes to and from the bus stop at Opéra Garnier on rue Scribe. (€9, about a one-hour trip). You can reach your final destination by taking the métro from the nearby Opéra métro station.

A **taxi** ride costs at least €40 to the city center. The price will be a bit higher than on the meter as a charge will be added for your baggage. At night, fares are up to 50% higher. You'll find the taxi line outside the terminals. It will frequently be long, but moves quite fast. Never take an unmetered taxi!

Minivan shuttles cost about €30 for two. One service is **Paris Airport Service**, www.parisairportservice.com, Tel. 01/55.98.10.80.

Orly has two terminals: Sud (south) for international flights, and Ouest (west) for domestic flights. A free shuttle bus connects the two. A taxi from Orly to the city costs about €35 and up to 50% more at night.

Orly Val is a monorail (stopping at both terminals) to the RER train station at Anthony (a ten-minute ride), then on to the city on the RER (Line B) train. The ride takes 30 minutes. The cost is €9 for both the monorail and the train ride.

GETTING AROUND PARIS

Car Rental
Are you crazy? Parking is chaotic, gas is extremely expensive, and driving in Paris is an unpleasant "adventure." With the incredible public transportation system in Paris, there's absolutely no reason to rent a car.

Métro (Subway)
The métro system is clearly the best way to get around Paris. It's orderly, inexpensive and for the most part safe. You're rarely far

from a métro station in Paris. They are marked by a **yellow "M"** in a circle, or ornate lamposts with a red **"Métro"** sign, or by those incredibly beautiful Art Nouveau archways with **"Métropolitain"** on them. Although you may be confused when you first look at a métro map, simply follow the line that your stop is on and note the last stop (the last stop appears on all the signs) and you'll soon be scurrying about underground like a Parisian. Service starts at 5:30am and ends between midnight and 1am (until 2am on Saturday night/Sunday mornings and the eve of holidays). Métro tickets are also valid on buses. Each ticket costs €1.40. Buy a *carnet* (10 tickets for about €11).

If you're staying in Paris for a longer period of time, a *carte orange* for zones 1 and 2 (Paris and nearby suburbs) costs about €16 a week or about €52 per month and allows unlimited use of both the métro and the bus system. You'll need a pass (you can get them at any major métro station) and a passport-size photo. That's why there are so many of those photo booths at stations. There are many options available for métro passes. Check them out. Keep your ticket throughout your trip. An inspector can fine you if you can't produce a stamped ticket.

Buses
Buses run from 6:30am to 8:30pm, with some night routes running until 12:30am. Bus routes are shown on the *Plan des Autobus*, a map available at métro stations. The route is shown at each bus stop. **You can use métro tickets on the bus**, but you can't switch between the bus and métro on the same ticket. Enter through the front door and validate your ticket in the machine behind the driver. You can also purchase a ticket from the driver. Exit out the back door.

If you'd like a quick tour of major sights, **bus #69** will take you from the Eiffel Tower passing the Seine River, the Louvre, through the Marais all the way to Père Lachaise Cemetery.

Taxis
You'll pay a minimum of €5 for a taxi ride. Fares are usually described in English on a sticker on the window. A typical 10-minute ride will cost around €10. There are taxi stands around the city, often near métro stops.

BASIC INFORMATION

Banking & Changing Money

The **euro (€)** is the currency of France and most of Europe. Before you leave for Paris, it's a good idea to get some euros. It makes your arrival a lot easier. Call your credit-card company or bank before you leave to tell them that you'll be using your ATM or credit card outside the country. Many have automatic controls that can "freeze" your account if the computer program determines that there are charges outside your normal area. ATMs (of course, with fees) are the easiest way to change money in Paris. You'll find them everywhere. You can still get traveler's checks, but why bother?

Business Hours

Shop hours vary, but generally are from 9:30am to 7:30pm from Monday through Saturday. Most shops are closed on Sunday. Many restaurants and shops close for the month of August.

Climate & Weather

Average high temperature/low temperature/days of rain:
- January: 43° F / 34° F / 10
- February: 45° / 34° / 9
- March: 51° / 38° / 10
- April: 57° / 42° / 9
- May: 64° / 48° / 10
- June: 70° / 54° / 9
- July: 75° / 58° / 8
- August: 75° / 57° / 7
- September: 69° / 52° / 9
- October: 59° / 46° / 10
- November: 49° / 39° / 10
- December: 45° / 36° / 11

Check www.weather.com before you leave.

Consulates & Embassies
- **US**: 1st / Métro Concorde, 2 rue St-Florentin, Tel. 01/43.12.22.22 or 01/43.12.23.47

• **Canada**: 8th/Métro Franklin-D. Roosevelt, 35 avenue Montaigne, Tel. 01/44.43.29.00

Electricity

The electrical current in Paris is 220 volts as opposed to 110 volts found at home. Don't fry your electric razor, hairdryer or laptop. You'll need a converter and an adapter. (Most laptops don't require a converter, but why are you bringing that anyway?)

Emergencies & Safety

Paris is one of the safest large cities in the world. Still, don't wear a "fanny pack;" it's a sign that you're a tourist and an easy target (especially in crowded tourist areas and the métro). Avoid wearing expensive jewelry in the métro.

Check with your health-care provider. Most policies don't cover you overseas. If that's the case, you may want to obtain medical insurance. Given the uncertainties in today's world, you may also want to purchase trip-cancellation insurance (for insurance coverage, check out www.insuremytrip.com). Make sure that your policy covers sickness, disasters, bankruptcy and State Department travel restrictions and warnings. In other words, read the fine print!

Festivals & Holidays

January: If you love shopping, it's time for post-holiday bargains. Parisians call it *"les soldes."* Paris is also host to the international ready-to-wear fashion shows held at the Parc des Expositions (15th).

February: The *Salon de l'Agriculture* showcases France's important agricultural industry. Included in the celebration are food and wine from throughout France.

French Holidays

- **New Year's**: January 1
- **Easter**
- **Ascension** (40 days after Easter)
- **Pentecost** (seventh Sunday after Easter)
- **May Day**: May 1
- **Victory in Europe**: May 8
- **Bastille Day**: July 14
- **Assumption of the Virgin Mary**: August 15
- **All Saints'**: November 1
- **Armistice**: November 11
- **Christmas**: December 25

March: At the end of the month is the *Foire du Trône*, a huge amusement park held at the Bois de Vincennes (12th). With Ferris wheels, circus attractions and carousels, it's like a sophisticated county fair.

April: Paris is home to the International Marathon. On the first weekend, spectators line the Champs-Élysées to watch the women's and men's marathons. Some of the best jazz artists come to Paris at the end of the month for the *Fête de Jazz*. Events and concerts featuring jazz artists are held throughout the city.

May: Tennis is king in late May as Paris hosts the French Open (they call it *"Roland Garros"*).

June: Music fills the air during the many concerts as part of the *Fête de la Musique*. From Guatemalan street musicians to serious opera, you'll be exposed to Paris's diversity. Most concerts are free.

July: In early July, Paris hosts a huge gay-pride parade. On the 14th, Parisians celebrate *Le Quatorze Juillet* or Bastille Day with city-wide celebrations, fireworks and a huge military parade down the Champs-Élysées. In late July, the *Tour de France* is completed when bikers ride down the Champs-Élysées. This is also a huge month for *soldes* (clothing sales).

August: Sunbathe, drink and celebrate the Seine River at *Paris-Plage*. Hundreds of deck chairs, umbrellas, cabanas and even

palm trees are all brought to the Right Bank of the river from Pont de Sully to Pont Neuf. You can enjoy the sun, have a drink or two and a snack. No, I don't recommend that you swim in the Seine. In the late afternoon and evening, musicians play along the river.

September: You can visit historical monuments (some of which are usually closed to the public) during *Fête du Patrimoine*. In late September, Paris again hosts the international ready-to-wear fashion convention at Parc des Expositions (15th).

October: Thousands of horse-racing fans arrive in Paris for the *Prix de l'Arc de Triomphe Lucien Barrière*. It's considered to be the ultimate thoroughbred horse race. It's held at the Hippodrome de Longchamps (16th).

November: Only in France would the arrival of wine be celebrated as a huge event. Get ready to drink **Beaujolais Nouveau** (a fruity wine from Burgundy) on the third Thursday.

December: A skating rink is installed in front of the **Hôtel de Ville** (City Hall). The large windows of the major department stores (Bon Marché, BHV, Galeries Lafayette and Printemps) are decorated in interesting (sometimes bizarre) Christmas themes. *Fête de St-Sylvestre* (New Year's Eve) is celebrated throughout the city. At midnight, the Eiffel Tower is a virtual light show and the city is filled with champagne-drinking Parisians welcoming the new year (and a few tourists hoping they'll return to this great city in the years to come).

Internet Access
Cyber cafés seem to pop up everywhere (and go out of business quickly). You shouldn't have difficulty finding a place to e-mail home. Remember that French keyboards are different than those found in the U.S. and Canada. The going rate is about €2 per hour.

Language
Please, make the effort to speak a little French. It will get you a long way — even if all you can say is *Parlez-vous anglais?* (par-lay voo ahn-glay): Do you speak English? Gone are the days when

Parisians were only interested in correcting your French. You'll find helpful French phrases in a few pages.

Passport Regulations

You'll need a **valid passport** to enter France. If you're staying more than 90 days, you must obtain a visa. Canadians don't need visas.

Citizens of the U.S. who have been away more than 48 hours can bring home $800 of merchandise duty-free every 30 days. For more information, go to Traveler Information ("Know Before You Go") at www.customs.gov. Canadians can bring back C$750 each year if gone for 7 days or more.

Hotel and restaurant prices are required by law to include taxes and service charges. **Value Added Tax** (VAT, or TVA in France) is nearly 20% (33% on luxury goods). The VAT is included in the price of goods (except services such as restaurants). Foreigners are entitled to a refund and must fill out a refund form. When you make your purchase, you should ask for the form and instructions if you're purchasing €182 or more in one place and in one day (no combining). Yes, it can be a hassle. Check out www.globalrefund.com for the latest information on refunds (and help for a fee).

Postal Services

Be prepared to wait in line. There is a post office at 52 rue du Louvre that's open 24 hours. There's also a main post office on the Champs-Élysées at #71. If you're mailing postcards, you can purchase stamps at many *tabacs* (tobacco shops) and stands that sell newspapers and postcards.

Restrooms

There aren't a lot of public restrooms. If you need to go, your best bet is to head (no pun intended) to the nearest café or brasserie. It's considered good manners to purchase something if you use the restroom. Some métro stations have public restrooms. Another option are those strange self-cleaning restrooms that look like some sort of pod found on some streets in Paris. Don't be shocked to walk into a restroom and find two porcelain footprints and a hole in the floor. These old "Turkish toilets" still exist. Hope you have strong thighs!

Smoking
There is now a smoking ban for all public places. Beginning in 2008, restaurants, hotels, bars-tabacs, and nightclubs must be smoke-free. If it can happen in Paris, it can happen anywhere.

Telephones
- Country code for France is 33
- Area code for Paris is 01
- Calls beginning with 0800 are toll-free
- Calling Paris from the U.S. and Canada: dial 011-33-1 plus the eight-digit local number. You drop the 0 in the area code
- Calling the U.S. or Canada from Paris: dial 00 (wait for the tone), dial 1 plus the area code and local number
- Calling within Paris: dial 01 and the eight-digit local number.

Phone cards are the cheapest way to call. Get one from many *tabacs*, métro stations or magazine kiosks.

A great way to stay in touch and save money is to **rent an international cell phone**. One provider is www.cellhire.com. Few cell phones purchased in the U.S. work in Europe. If you're a frequent visitor to Europe, you may want to purchase a cell phone (for about $50) from www.mobal.com. You'll get an international telephone number and pay by the minute for calls made on your cell phone.

Time
When it's noon in New York City, it's 6pm in Paris. For hours of events or schedules, the French use the 24-hour clock. So 6am is 0600 and 1pm is 1300.

Tipping
See the *Best Eats* section in chapter 7 for tipping in restaurants. Other tips: 10% for taxi drivers, €1 for room service, €1.50 per bag to the hotel porter, €1.50 per day for maid service and up to €.50 to bathroom attendants.

Tourist Information

The main tourist information office is on the Champs-Élysées at 127. It's open daily from 9am to 8pm, and is usually crowded. Both airports have offices. There are also offices at the Gare de Lyon train station (open daily 9am-8pm), the Louvre (open Wed-Mon 10am-7pm) and the Eiffel Tower (open daily May-Sept 11am-6:30pm). There's also an office at Charles de Gaulle (terminal 2F), open daily 9am- 8pm.

Water

Tap water is safe in Paris. Occasionally, you'll find *non potable* signs in restrooms. This means that the water is not safe for drinking.

Web Sites

- Paris Tourist Office: www.parisinfo.com
- French Government Tourist Office: www.franceguide.com
- U.S. State Department: www.travel.state.gov

ESSENTIAL FRENCH PHRASES

please, *s'il vous plait* (seel voo *play*)
thank you, *merci* (*mair* see)
yes, *oui* (wee)
no, *non* (nohn)
good morning, *bonjour* (bohn *jhoor*)
good afternoon, *bonjour* (bohn *jhoor*)
good evening, *bonsoir* (bohn *swahr*)
goodbye, *au revoir* (o ruh *vwahr*)
sorry/excuse me, *pardon* (pahr-*dohn*)
you are welcome, *de rien* (duh ree *ehn*)

do you speak English?, *parlez-vous anglais?* (par lay voo ahn *glay*)
I don't speak French, *je ne parle pas français* (jhuh ne parl pah frahn *say*)
I don't understand, *je ne comprends pas* (jhuh ne kohm *prahn* pas)
I'd like a table, *je voudrais une table* (zhuh voo *dray* ewn tabl)
I'd like to reserve a table, *je voudrais réserver une table* (zhuh voo *dray* rayzehrvay ewn tabl)

for one, *pour un* (poor oon),two, *deux* (duh), *trois* (twah)(3), *quatre* (*kaht*-ruh)(4),*cinq* (sank)(5), *six* (cease)(6), *sept* (set)(7), *huit* (wheat)(8), *neuf* (nerf)(9), *dix* (dease)(10)

waiter/sir, *monsieur* (muh-*syuh*) (never *garçon*!)

waitress/miss, *mademoiselle* (mad mwa *zel*)

knife, *couteau* (koo *toe*)

spoon, *cuillère* (kwee *air*)

fork, *fourchette* (four *shet*)

menu, *la carte* (la cart) (not *menu*!)

wine list, *la carte des vins* (la *cart* day van)

no smoking, *défense de fumer* (day *fahns* de fu may)

toilets, *les toilettes* (lay twa *lets*)

closed, *fermé* (fehr-may)

open, *ouvert* (oo-vehr)

today, *aujourd'hui* (o zhoor *dwee*)

tomorrow, *demain* (duh *mehn*)

tonight, *ce soir* (suh *swahr*)

Monday, *lundi* (luhn *dee*)

Tuesday, *mardi* (mahr *dee*)

Wednesday, *mercredi* (mair kruh *dee*)

Thursday, *jeudi* (jheu *dee*)

Friday, *vendredi* (vawn druh *dee*)

Saturday, *samedi* (sahm *dee*)

Sunday, *dimanche* (dee *mahnsh*)

here, *ici* (ee-*see*)

there, *là* (la)

what, *quoi* (kwah)

when, *quand* (kahn)

where, *où est* (ooh-eh)

how much, *c'est combien* (say comb bee *ehn*)

credit cards, *les cartes de crédit* (lay kart duh creh *dee*)

INDEX